Methodology to Improve Control Plane Security in SDN Environments

T0271835

Published 2024 by River Publishers

River Publishers

Alsbjergvej 10, 9260 Gistrup, Denmark

www.riverpublishers.com

Distributed exclusively by Routledge

605 Third Avenue, New York, NY 10017, USA

4 Park Square, Milton Park, Abingdon, Oxon OX14 4RN

Methodology to Improve Control Plane Security in SDN Environments / by Wendwossen Desalegn, Javed Shaikh, Bayisa Taye.

Routledge is an imprint of the Taylor & Francis Group, an informa business

ISBN 978-87-7004-195-9 (paperback)

ISBN 978-87-7004-219-2 (online)

ISBN 978-8-770-04212-3 (ebook master)

A Publication in the River Publishers Series in Rapids

While every effort is made to provide dependable information, the publisher, authors, and editors cannot be held responsible for any errors or omissions.

Methodology to Improve Control Plane Security in SDN Environments

Wendwossen Desalegn

Adama Science and Technology University, Ethiopia

Javed Shaikh

Adama Science and Technology University, Ethiopia

Bayisa Taye

Adama Science and Technology University, Ethiopia

Routledge
Taylor & Francis Group

NEW YORK AND LONDON

Contents

Preface

In today's digital landscape, software-defined networking (SDN) stands as a revolutionary architectural framework, streamlining network management by decoupling the data plane from the control plane. This pivotal separation not only simplifies network deployment but also furnishes a programmable interface for application development, particularly in critical domains like security management. Central to this paradigm is the centralized logical controller, offering unparalleled oversight across the network, affording complete visibility.

This book chronicles an exhaustive study aimed at crafting a robust security solution tailored for the SDN environment, specifically targeting the detection and mitigation of distributed denial of service (DDoS) attacks on the control plane. The proposed methodology hinges on an early detection strategy, meticulously aligned with industry standards, serving as a beacon for professionals navigating the intricate realm of security solutions implementation. This ook elucidates an innovative approach devised to identify and mitigate the inherent risks associated with the OpenFlow protocol and its POX controller. Validated through rigorous simulations conducted within controlled environments utilizing the Mininet tool and SDN controller, the methodology unfolds, showcasing the intricate dance between theory and practice.

Through meticulous observation of detection algorithm results in simulated environments, followed by real-world implementation within network testbeds, the proposed solution emerges triumphant. Leveraging network entropy calculation, coupled with swift port blocking mechanisms, the methodology stands as a formidable barrier against a DDoS attack such as TCP, UDP, and ICMP floods.

Embark on a journey of discovery, as this book unveils the blueprint for safeguarding the very backbone of modern communication networks. With unparalleled clarity and insight, it offers a roadmap towards fortifying SDN infrastructures against the relentless onslaught of cyber threats, ensuring resilience and reliability in an ever-evolving digital landscape.

About the Authors

Wendwossen Desalegn earned a Bachelor's degree in electrical and computer engineering from Hawassa University in Ethiopia in 2016 and a Master's degree in electronic and communication engineering from Adama Science and Technology University (ASTU) in 2022. He is a cyber security specialist and network engineer who has designed and implemented firewalls and holds CCNA and CCNP certifications. Currently, he works with IPCOM Technologies in Addis Ababa, Ethiopia. He has over 6 years of experience in this industry. His research interests are cybersecurity, SDN, SDS, and network automation.

Javed Shaikh received his Bachelor of Engineering degree in electronics and telecommunications from Dr. BAMU University, India in 2009 and Master of Engineering degree in VLSI and embedded systems from Pune University in 2012. He received his PhD degree in Communication and Computer Engineering from Technical University of Sofia (TUS), Bulgaria. Currently, he is working with the Department of Electronics and Communication Engineering, Adama Science and Technology University, Adama, Ethiopia and as an Assistant Professor. He has 13+ years of teaching experience of teaching in India and abroad. His research interests include communication networks, cryptography, AI and ML, cyber security and E-commerce systems, and 5G networks. He has published several papers in reputed journals and conferences.

Bayisa Taye Mulatu received his Bachelor of Science degree in electrical and computer engineering from Addis Ababa University, Ethiopia in 2009 and Master of Engineering degree in computer science and communication engineering from Waseda University, Japan, in 2018. Previously he worked at Ethio Telecom, as network engineer and later in public universities: Hawassa University, Dilla University and Bule Hora University. Currently, he is working with the Department of Electronics and Communication Engineering, Adama

Science and Technology University, Adama, Ethiopia and he is serving as a Lecturer. His research interests include wireless communication networks, cloud computing, AI and ML, and 5G and beyond-5G networks. He has published several papers in reputed journals and conferences.

List of Abbreviations

API	Application programming interface
CPU	Central processing unit
CRT	Commercial remote terminal
DDoS	Distributed denial of service
ICMP	Internet control message protocol
IDS	Intrusion detection system
IP	Internet protocol
LTS	Long term service
NFV	Network functions virtualization
NOS	Network operating system
NVMe	Non-volatile memory express
ONF	Open networking foundation
OSI	Open systems interconnection
OVS	Open virtual switch
PoC	Proof of concept
SDN	Software defined networking
SSD	Solid state drive
TCP	Transmission control protocol
TLS	Transport layer security
UDP	User datagram protocol
VM	Virtual machine
WAN	Wide area network

1

Introduction

This chapter contains critical realm of control plane security within the context of software-defined networking (SDN). As the central intelligence and command center of an SDN environment, the control plane holds immense power and vulnerability. Building upon a foundational understanding of software defined security (SDS) and SDN, this chapter dives deeper into the specific threats and attack vectors targeting the control plane. You will learn about authentication weaknesses, configuration errors and other exploitable aspects, explore sophisticated attacks like distributed denial of service (DDoS) and malware specifically targeting the control plane and discover best practices for securing the control plane, including access controls, encryption, and intrusion detection/prevention systems.

This chapter serves as a valuable guide for IT professionals and security practitioners navigating the increasingly complex world of SDN. By understanding the unique security challenges of the control plane, you can implement effective measures to ensure the stability and integrity of your network.

1.1 The Evolution of SDS (Software Defined Security)

In the dynamic landscape of network security, there exists an ongoing race, a relentless competition between adversaries and security communities, each vying to outpace the other in breaking and fortifying the network. The diligent efforts of security researchers and practitioners have yielded commendable progress in mitigating threats posed by adversaries. Yet, the rapid proliferation of information and communication technologies, including the ubiquity of mobile devices and the paradigm shift brought about by cloud computing virtualization, introduces a fresh set of challenges for network administrators. The continuous evolution of technology gives rise to new vulnerabilities, sophisticated attack mechanisms, and novel attack channels. Compounded by the escalating industry demand and the surge in cloud services, the conventional model, intricately dependent on each provider with its inconsistent policies, becomes both unscalable and impractical. In response to this pressing need, researchers in the realm of network solutions have innovatively crafted a response—a groundbreaking technology known as software-defined networking (SDN).

When delving into the intersection of security and software-defined networking (SDN), two distinct perspectives emerge. Initially, the book considered security within the context of SDN, exploring the novel benefits that the fusion of these realms could yield and how it redefines the landscape of SDN security. The layered structure inherent in SDN emphasizes the imperative that each stratum within the SDN model maintains its individual security integrity. The resilience of any security system hinges on the strength of its weakest link, a principle underscored by the multiple layers intrinsic to an SDN implementation.

Emphasizing the crucial role of security in all network designs, be it conventional or SDN-based architectures, this book highlights how SDN can be a facilitator for provisioning and enforcing robust security plans. It is reiterated that the security efficacy of an SDN scheme is contingent upon addressing vulnerabilities across the three concentrated planes or layers: application, control, and data. Noteworthy advantages of SDN in security management include effective monitoring of abnormal traffic and prompt mitigation of vulnerabilities.

The pervasive presence of SDN across personal, national, and hybrid cloud networks, coupled with the distributed nature of web operations teams, presents a diverse landscape for companies across industries. As organizations transition from reactive to preventive system management, the article suggests the critical role of performance monitoring. Standard measures become indispensable to identify resource utilization issues before they impact the system. Amidst this technological evolution, web safety, especially concerning the vast expanse of the internet, emerges as a prominent data security concern.

Educational institutions are at varying stages of integrating their technology resources into unified systems, prompting considerations about connecting personal networks with trusted users to the broader and potentially riskier internet community. Regardless of the deployment model, SDN plays a pivotal role in providing perimeter security, reshaping the traditional concept of a single boundary into a more nuanced and distributed security paradigm. In an era where any IP-based device connected to a network can pose a potential threat, securing each network element or function within an organization becomes imperative. This multifaceted security approach, termed SDN security, requires secure boundaries around services and access, treating each layer within an implementation as if it had its own distinct perimeter. As organizations navigate the complexities of SDN, they must weigh the costs and benefits of establishing connections across diverse network landscapes, adapting their security postures to the evolving realities of the Internet of Everything.

In the ever-evolving landscape of cybersecurity, the paradigm shift towards software-defined security (SDS) stands as a testament to the need for adaptive, responsive, and dynamic defense mechanisms. As we delve into the roots of software-defined security, we find ourselves tracing a transformative journey from traditional security models to the contemporary, software-centric approach that is redefining how we safeguard our digital realms. In the early days of cybersecurity, traditional models relied heavily on hardware-centric solutions, such as firewalls and intrusion detection systems. These approaches, while foundational, began to reveal their limitations in the face of increasingly sophisticated threats. The static nature of hardware-based defenses struggled to keep pace with the dynamic and agile strategies employed by cyber adversaries.

The turning point came with the rise of software-defined networking (SDN). As organizations sought more flexibility and control over their network infrastructure, the software-defined approach gained prominence. SDN introduced the concept of separating the network control plane from the data plane, paving the way for centralized, programmable network management. It wasn't long before security considerations became intertwined with this software-defined ethos. The fusion of SDN and security gave birth to software-defined security, a paradigm that transcended the constraints of traditional models. SDS brought with it a new set of principles, emphasizing adaptability, scalability, and the ability to respond dynamically to emerging threats. The static, rule-based security of the past gave way to policies that could be shaped and adjusted in real-time, offering a level of agility previously unseen in cybersecurity.

One of the key milestones in the evolution of SDS was its seamless integration with cloud environments. As organizations embraced cloud computing, the need for security measures that could match the scalability and dynamism of virtualized environments became paramount. SDS stepped up to the challenge, offering security solutions that could operate natively in virtualized and cloud-native ecosystems.

Automation and orchestration emerged as crucial components of SDS, introducing the concept of dynamic threat response. Automated processes could analyze threats in real-time and trigger immediate, adaptive responses, reducing the window of vulnerability. Orchestrating security policies across diverse environments became not just a convenience but a necessity in the face of an increasingly interconnected digital landscape.

SDS also welcomed the integration of threat intelligence, leveraging real-time data to enhance its proactive defense mechanisms. The ability to adapt security postures based on the ever-shifting threat landscape became a hallmark of SDS implementations. This fusion of intelligence and dynamic policy enforcement elevated the overall efficacy of cybersecurity measures.

As we reflect on the journey so far, numerous case studies stand as testament to the success of SDS implementations. Industries across the spectrum, from finance to healthcare, have witnessed tangible improvements in agility and security efficacy. SDS has proven its worth as not just a theoretical advancement but a practical solution to the evolving challenges of cybersecurity.

However, this evolution hasn't been without its challenges. Interoperability hurdles and the delicate balance between automation and human oversight pose ongoing considerations for those venturing into the realm of SDS. Yet, these challenges are not roadblocks but rather milestones in the continued maturation of this transformative approach to cybersecurity.

Looking ahead, the future of software-defined security appears poised for further integration with emerging technologies such as artificial intelligence and blockchain. The adaptive nature of SDS aligns seamlessly with the demands of an ever-changing digital landscape, making it a vanguard in the ongoing battle against cyber threats.

In conclusion, the evolution of software-defined security represents a compelling narrative of innovation and resilience in the face of evolving cyber threats. From the static defenses of the past to the dynamic, software-defined security measures of today, this journey exemplifies the adaptability and ingenuity required to stay ahead in the complex and ever-shifting world of cybersecurity. As we continue to explore new frontiers, software-defined security stands ready to shape the future of digital defense.

In the relentless pursuit of fortifying our digital fortresses, the evolution of SDS has been a symphony of innovation, resilience, and adaptive intelligence. Beyond the binary world of traditional security models, SDS ushered in an era where defense mechanisms could dance to the dynamic rhythm of the ever-evolving threat landscape.

The historical context reveals a narrative where early attempts at software-centric security were met with skepticism and caution. Legacy firewalls and intrusion detection systems, while foundational, proved to be rigid structures in the face of the relentless march of cyber threats. The realization dawned that a more agile, responsive approach was required to counter the sophistication and agility of contemporary adversaries.

Enter software-defined networking (SDN), a technological evolution that would inadvertently shape the destiny of cybersecurity. As organizations sought to break free from the shackles of hardware-centric limitations, SDN emerged as the harbinger of change. The separation of the control plane and data plane not only revolutionized network management but also laid the groundwork for a security paradigm where adaptability was paramount.

The birth of software-defined security was akin to introducing a thinking, learning element into the static realm of cybersecurity. It represented a seismic shift from predefined rules to policies that could morph and adapt in real-time. This adaptability became the cornerstone of SDS, allowing security measures to evolve alongside the ever-shifting tactics of cyber adversaries.

Cloud environments became both the testing ground and the proving ground for SDS. As organizations embraced the scalability and flexibility offered by cloud computing, SDS seamlessly integrated itself into these virtualized landscapes. The result was security that could not only keep pace with the rapid expansion of digital footprints but also anticipate and mitigate threats before they could manifest.

Automation and orchestration became the dynamic duo of SDS, introducing a level of efficiency and responsiveness previously unattainable. The ability to automate routine security tasks liberated human resources to focus on strategic, high-level analysis. Simultaneously, orchestration ensured a symphonic coordination of security policies across diverse environments, harmonizing the defense posture.

The marriage of SDS with threat intelligence elevated cybersecurity to a new echelon of sophistication. Real-time analysis of threat data allowed SDS implementations to not merely respond to current threats but anticipate and prepare for future ones. This predictive capability became a force multiplier, enabling organizations to stay ahead of the curve in an environment where the only constant is change.

Numerous success stories stand as testament to the practical impact of SDS. Industries facing diverse challenges, from financial institutions navigating complex regulatory landscapes to healthcare organizations safeguarding sensitive patient data, have found SDS to be not just a solution but a strategic ally in the battle against cyber threats.

Challenges persist, as they always do in the realm of innovation. Interoperability concerns and the delicate dance between automated responses and human oversight continue to shape the ongoing narrative of SDS. However, these challenges are not stumbling blocks but rather the crucible in which SDS continues to refine its form and function.

As we gaze into the future, the trajectory of SDS seems poised for even greater heights. The integration of emerging technologies like artificial intelligence and blockchain promises to further fortify the defenses. The adaptive nature of SDS positions it as a linchpin in the cybersecurity landscape, capable of navigating uncharted territories in the perpetual cat-and-mouse game with cyber threats.

In conclusion, the evolution of SDS is more than a technological tale; it's a saga of resilience, adaptability, and the relentless pursuit of security in a digital world fraught with challenges. From the early days of skepticism to the current landscape of dynamic, intelligent defense, SDS exemplifies the spirit of innovation required to navigate the complex and ever-shifting currents of cybersecurity. As we stand at the cusp of tomorrow, SDS beckons as a beacon, guiding the way forward in the ongoing quest for digital resilience.

1.1.1 Security for the SDN

The convergence of security and software-defined networks (SDNs) encompasses specific objectives, particularly in the realm of SDNs and security. Departing from the conventional overlay model, SDN design allows for the seamless embedding of security within the network fabric. This integration is not contingent upon the SDN model, ensuring a versatile approach to security regardless of the specific model employed.

Several advantageous features arise from this integration, including centralized policy administration, automatic provisioning, real-time mitigation, and the ability to execute security checks during the implementation of network configurations. These benefits are inherent to SDN, crafted from the ground up, and intrinsic to its foundational structure.

However, as security is a paramount concern in all network models, the evolving threat landscape introduces variations in the effects of common network attacks within an SDN system. Recognizing this, a learning curve emerges concerning the application and emergence of dangers within an SDN network. For instance, the dynamics of a distributed denial of service (DDoS) attack differ in an SDN context, where attackers may focus on manipulating flow information on a single device, triggering a cascade effect across the network.

The success of such tactics relies heavily on the security posture of the SDN. Given its layered architecture, each level demands a unique security approach. SDN security introduces novel potential threats and vulnerabilities, necessitating a multi-layered security strategy tailored to the multi-component nature of SDN models.

The control plane emerges as the vital core of an SDN network, connecting network devices and applications. Controllers, utilizing open flow protocols like OpenFlow, configure network devices and optimize paths for application traffic. Controller hardening strategies aim to shield against access-based attacks and misconfigurations. Meanwhile, operating systems on the controller must be meticulously patched and maintained.

Authentication, authorization, and accounting (AAA) with role-based access control play a pivotal role in monitoring and auditing configured entities on control-enabled hosts. Security by design extends to control-specific hardening, ensuring that SDN agents and other devices receiving commands are fortified against potential threats.

The data plane security approach is imperative, rejecting unwanted traffic promptly to safeguard device resources. Network services are secured by defining and adhering to a network security policy, allowing only essential services while mitigating potential vulnerabilities. The control of applications and APIs is addressed through secure coding practices, and threat management protocols are implemented around SDN agents.

In the context of SDN deployments, legacy network security concerns persist, prompting the transfer of static firewalls and middlebox appliances onto SDN architectures. Centralizing control on the SDN controller necessitates meticulous security measures to prevent network failures due to a single point of failure. The security of the SDN controller is multidimensional, covering various entry points that hackers might exploit, and must be comprehensively reviewed in light of primary attack vectors influencing SDN architectural integration points across distinct planes.

1.1.2 Security by the SDN

SDN agents and controllers can be strategically configured to function as a perimeter safeguarding specific devices or services. Security services integrated into agent systems enable the application of identity management, threat defense, content inspection, and compliance measures. These services extend to connections and forms, ensuring adherence to regulatory requirements. Controllers are assigned the responsibility of identifying and responding to attacks and anomalies, enforcing network-wide containment, and disseminating crucial protection upgrades.

Post-deployment, challenges related to security policy provisioning are efficiently addressed, and the monitoring of performance becomes centralized and automated. While configuring a feature, it becomes imperative to conduct checks for the correct policy, accurate configuration, and proper syntax. Performing a configuration check before passing it down to an agent is crucial to ensure that the configuration is error-free. This step is vital as service disruptions or attacks may not always stem from external threats but can also result from simple configuration issues.

Attacks and abnormalities are promptly reported to controllers, empowering them to implement network-wide containment measures and disseminate security updates. The proactive protection of agents upon the detection of an attack is instrumental in restricting or eliminating the impact of DDoS-type attacks on the network.

A fundamental aspect of SDN security lies in its inherent integration into the deployment process from the outset. It transcends the concept of an overlay, becoming an integral component of core technology. Notably, the layered approach in a typical SDN implementation exemplifies the systematic integration of security. Once the containment and mitigation strategy is transmitted to the SDN layer, it cascades to other agents within the network. Upon completion, the result is enterprise-wide protection, with policy updates seamlessly distributed to all network agents. This holistic approach ensures that security is not an afterthought but an integral and embedded element of the entire SDN ecosystem.

1.2 Introduction to SDN (Software-defined Networking)

SDN stands as an innovative networking technology designed to revolutionize traditional network architectures, providing enhanced flexibility and scalability.

Figure 1.1: Traditional and SDN approaches (Stallings, 2015).

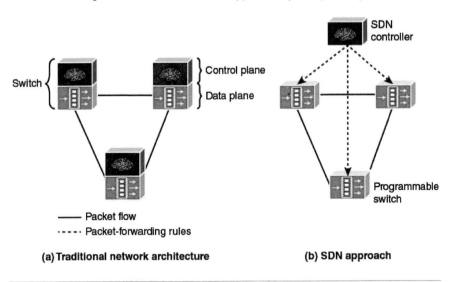

(a) Traditional network architecture   (b) SDN approach

This transformative approach allows for swift adaptation to changes in business requirements and end-user needs through simplified network management, as noted by Mladenov (2019). Demonstrating its prowess, SDN has seamlessly extended its reach from small local area networks to encompass expansive public cloud architectures. In various scenarios, SDN has proven its success by delivering heightened reliability, efficiency, simplicity, and flexibility—all achieved at a reduced cost, as highlighted by Kandoi and Antikainen (2015). However, despite these compelling advantages, the security of SDN remains a focal point of concern within research communities.

The emergence of SDN addresses and eliminates the constraints that plagued traditional networks. Traditional networks grappled with issues such as complexity, reliance on vendor-specific languages for configuring individual devices, a lack of a holistic network view, and centralized control points, as articulated by Jose et al. (2021). Figure 1.1 shows the basic architectures of traditional networks and SDNs.

With the advent of SDNs, a paradigm shift occurred, enabling a comprehensive, global view of the network. This shift facilitates simplified network configuration and management, marking a departure from the intricacies of traditional setups.

At the core of SDN architecture is the pivotal separation of the control plane and the data plane—a defining characteristic of this technology. The logical centralization of control is embodied in a controller, often referred to as the network's brain. This controller serves as the operating system for the network, rendering it programmable through high-level languages. The SDN architecture, as elucidated by Jose et al. (2021), fosters a network environment that is easily configurable, manageable, and programmable, fundamentally transforming the landscape of modern networking.

1.2.1 SDN architecture

SDN is a network architecture that allows network engineers to dynamically initiate, control, alter, and manage network behavior using open interfaces such as the protocol OpenFlow. SDN is changing the way IT network infrastructures are managed, controlled, and configured (Lawal and Nuray, 2018). The SDN perspective is based on the separation of the control plane and the data plane, with one making data forwarding decisions and the other carrying them out. The non-control plane, like the SDN architecture, is managed by all network flow forwarding choices being made by a centralized controller.

The Open Networking Foundation (ONF) specifies the OpenFlow protocol is used to communicate between the two planes. The SDN architecture is comprised of three planes, as seen in Figure 1.2: the application plane, the control plane, and the data plane. In the SDN architecture, the control plane is made up of an SDN controller, which is a separated function from the data plane. The data plane is made up of packet forwarding hardware like routers, switches, and middlebox appliances (intrusion detection systems, load balancers, and firewalls). The SDN controller communicates with packet forwarding switches via open-source protocols such as OpenFlow. The OpenFlow protocol will dynamically deploy settings and rules to OpenFlow enabled switches on the packet forwarding plane (Kodzai, 2020). According to Bannour et al. (2017), the SDN application plane includes SDN applications or programs designed to implement network logic and control strategies.

A northbound API is used by this top-level plane to communicate with the control plane. SDN applications communicate network requirements to the SDN controller, which translates them into southbound-specific commands and forwarding rules that define the behavior of individual data plane devices. Routing, traffic engineering (TE), firewalls, and load balancing are examples of common SDN applications that run on top of existing controller platforms. The control plane, on the other hand, is considered the primary layer in the

Figure 1.2: SDN layered architecture (Stallings, 2015).

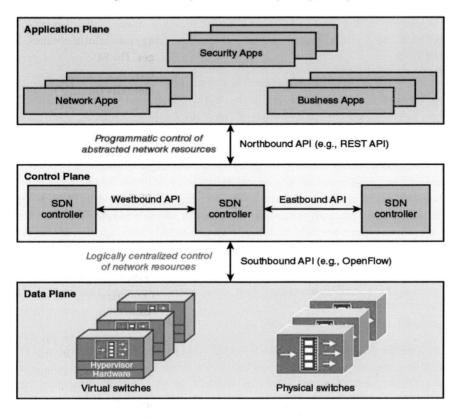

SDN architecture; it consists of a centralized software console that controls application and system communications network devices via open interfaces (Bannour et al., 2017). It also offers centralized management functions such as topology discovery, state synchronization, and device management. It also allows the installation of third-party programs or applications.

The control SDN is also known as a network operating system (NOS), and it already supports network control logic and gives an abstract picture of the global network to the application layer, containing the information needed to establish time-based rules (Bannour et al., 2017).

The control plane is regarded as the "brain" (Kreutz et al., 2014). It is in control of all decisions and configuration updates supplied to packet forwarding devices in an SDN-based network. The control plane will contain the SDN controller, whose security is a vital component of this study. The SDN controller contains the rules set, logic, and decisions that are forwarded to the data plane via the OpenFlow protocol's southbound API. As a natural outcome, it has evolved into a vital component that governs the entire network (Kreutz et al., 2013).

Data plane (infrastructure layer) is a group of network devices that provide packet forwarding services on the network. The packet forwarding devices can be hardware or software-based, and they are dynamically configured once the controller sends configuration rules. The configuration rules are broadcast over the SDN controller's southbound interfaces using the OpenFlow protocol. The packet forwarding devices will be routers, switches, or appliances similar to those used in legacy networks, but without embedded control network intelligence. In legacy networks, routers make packet forwarding decisions based primarily on the destination IP address, whereas in SDN, packet forwarding actions are determined by flows of packets between both source and destination devices (Kodzai, 2020).

The southbound interface is an application programmable interface that defines the set of instructions sent to packet forwarding devices via the OpenFlow protocol. They serve as bridges between packet forwarding devices and control devices (Anthony, 2015).

The northbound interface is the application programmable interface in the architecture that interacts with northbound applications. The interface enables the deployment of middleboxes as services in the SDN architecture, load balancers, intrusion detection systems, and routing algorithms are examples (Anthony, 2015).

1.2.2 SDN controllers

The SDN controller is the heart (Anthony, 2015) of the SDN network, containing centralized logic, a policy database, and all the rules required to carry out predetermined actions on traffic flows passing via the forwarding plane. The SDN controller enables the SDN network to be programmable and to dynamically react to changing network circumstances. Several SDN controllers have been launched by various manufacturers, and some are currently being upgraded utilizing various programming languages like as C++, Python, and Java. The programming languages have benefits and drawbacks, with Python-based controllers having issues with multithreading and C++-based controllers having issues with memory management (Hadi et al., 2018). Beacon, RYU, NOX, POX, Floodlight, Maestro, and Open Daylight are examples of SDN controllers. Because of its better documentation and flexibility, the Python-based Open

Daylight project will be used as the SDN controller in the experimental setup for this book (Kreutz et al., 2014). Because it is one of the industry standards that was initially used by prominent companies such as Huawei and Cisco, the controller is the recommended SDN controller. Simply said, as traffic flows on the data plane, the SDN controller will have flows designed either proactively or reactively. The controller will have pre-installed rules in proactive mode before traffic enters the network. Reactive mode flows are implemented when unknown traffic is recognized and goes via the data plane network. Salman et al. (2016) analyzes numerous SDN controller modules.

The routing service module's topology manager and link discoverable node will be in charge of detecting and maintaining the state of the links between the controller and the packet forwarding switches through the OpenFlow protocol. (Salman et al., 2016). SDN controllers may be utilized in large networks in dispersed topologies to increase resilience, capacity, and network system uptime (Kalkan and Zeadally, 2017). By distributing the control function, the distributed solution can be capitalized as a security enhancement that reduces system outage and scaling limitations. The controller performs various tasks

Figure 1.3: SDN controller communication interfaces (Latif et al., 2020).

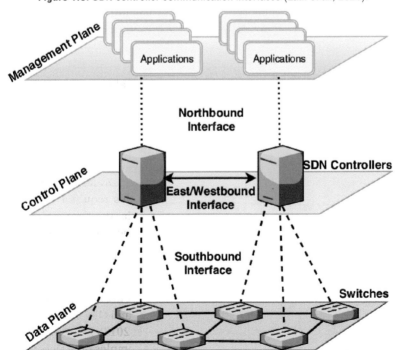

such as identifying network devices and their capabilities, collecting network statistics, and so on. Add-ons such as network monitoring and traffic anomaly detection can be used to extend and improve controller functionality. As shown in Figure 1.3, SDN controllers communicate via four interfaces: southbound, northbound, eastbound, and westbound. The controller uses the northbound channel to communicate with the application layer and the southbound channel to communicate with the infrastructure layer. The eastbound and westbound interfaces are used to allow communication between controllers (Haque et al., 2017).

1.2.3 SDN open virtual switches (OVSs)

The OVSs are positioned in the data plane of the SDN architecture and are responsible for the open system interconnection (OSI) model IP layer 2 and 3 packet forwarding activities on the user plane. The OpenFlow OVS switch has one or more tables with decision making rules (Salman et al., 2016). Data flows are forwarded based on predefined rules that can be changed as packets travel through the network.

As shown in Figure 1.4, the southbound interface on OVSs connects to the SDN controller and supports the standard OpenFlow protocol. OVSs are important because they provide benefits such as traffic filtering, quality of

Figure 1.4: OpenFlow message flow (Kodzai, 2020).

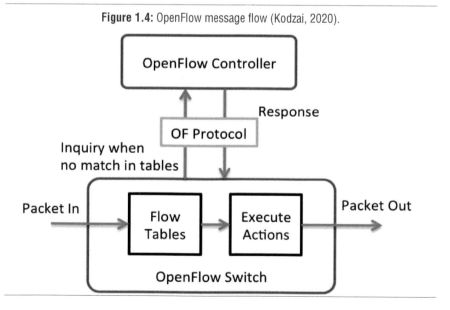

service, and some amount of security by dividing traffic into virtual local area network tags.

1.2.4 SDN OpenFlow protocol

The OpenFlow protocol is widely used in the current SDN; it is in charge of secure channel communication between the OpenFlow switch and the OpenFlow controller. The OpenFlow controller manages a flow table that contains a match field and flows instructions. The OpenFlow switch manages its flow table, which is supplied by the OpenFlow controller. OpenFlow defines both the communications protocol between the SDN data plane and the SDN control plane, as well as part of the behavior of the data plane. OpenFlow is a widely accepted and used technology for implementing and deploying SDN technology in today's networks. OpenFlow specifies how a centralized software driver communicates with a network forwarding device, and it provides a unified view of the network. Network policies and services are implemented as OpenFlow applications, which communicate with the control plane via the control plane's northbound API. The switch and the controller communicate via a transport layer security (TLS) enabled channel. Each switch, according to the specification, must have one or more flow tables that will maintain the flow inputs specified by the controller.

OpenFlow is a key standard communication protocol defined by the Open Network Foundation (ONF) that operates on the OVS's southbound interface to the SDN controller (Kodzai, 2020). In the event of new data plane traffic detection, the protocol enables dynamic flow table updating in OVSs. OpenFlow is a TCP/IP-based transport mechanism that operates on ports 6633 and 6653. The three primary forms of OpenFlow messages are described in Kodzai (2020). It may be characterized as controller to switch flow (asynchronous) started by the controller, asynchronous from the switches to the controller, and symmetric messages sent in both directions without solicitation (Kreutz et al., 2014).

The OVS OpenFlow operation entails recursive packet matching in a series of flow tables. Packet matching is performed by predefined priority tags, which determine the actions and rules that will be applied to traffic, such as discarding, blocking, forwarding, or changing (Kreutz et al., 2014). If there is no rule match in the OVS, the table that analyzes the flows is called the table miss flow entry (Kodzai, 2020), and it is configurable with options to drop the packet, send it to the controller, or push it to the follow table. The flow tables of the OVSs are scanned sequentially until the last table with 0 priority is reached, which determines the last potential action that may be done to that packet. Because of the use of OpenFlow, the controller becomes a primary target for the attacker as there is no standard for security implementation in the OpenFlow protocol and SDNs are programmable so they are much more vulnerable to a wide range of malicious attacks and code exploits.

1.3 The Significance of Control Plane Security

The control plane in networking refers to the component responsible for managing and controlling the flow of data within a network. It plays a crucial role in ensuring that network devices operate efficiently and effectively. Control plane security is a critical aspect of overall network security, as it focuses on protecting the mechanisms that govern the behavior of network devices. Here are some key points highlighting the significance of control plane security.

1.3.1 Network stability, reliability and role of network devices

The control plane is responsible for managing routing protocols, updating routing tables, and making decisions about how data should be forwarded within the network. Securing the control plane ensures the stability and reliability of the network by preventing unauthorized access or malicious manipulation that could disrupt routing decisions and lead to network instability.

Network devices, such as routers and switches, actively participate in the control plane by exchanging routing information and making decisions about how to forward traffic. Securing these devices involves implementing access controls, using secure management protocols (e.g., SSH), and regularly updating device firmware to patch vulnerabilities.

1.3.2 Preventing unauthorized access

Unauthorized access to the control plane can have severe consequences, such as eavesdropping on routing information, injecting malicious routing updates, or even taking control of network devices. Implementing control plane security measures, such as access control lists (ACLs) and authentication mechanisms, helps prevent unauthorized entities from compromising the control plane.

Utilizing secure management protocols for accessing and configuring network devices is crucial. Protocols like SSH (Secure Shell) should be preferred over insecure alternatives like Telnet. Encrypting management traffic ensures the confidentiality of sensitive information, such as login credentials and configuration details.

1.3.3 Protection against DoS attacks

Control plane security is essential for safeguarding against denial of service (DoS) attacks that specifically target the control plane of network devices. Attackers may flood the control plane with excessive traffic, overwhelming the processing capacity and causing disruptions. By implementing security measures, such as rate limiting and filtering, organizations can mitigate the impact of such attacks.

Implementing traffic filtering mechanisms on network devices helps control the types and volumes of traffic allowed to reach the control plane. Rate limiting can be used to restrict the number of control plane messages processed per unit of time, mitigating the impact of potential DoS attacks.

1.3.4 Ensuring protocol integrity and SIEM

Many network protocols operate within the control plane, and their integrity is crucial for proper network functioning. Security mechanisms, including digital signatures and message authentication codes, can be employed to ensure the authenticity and integrity of control plane messages, protecting against malicious tampering.

Integrating SIEM solutions into the network infrastructure allows organizations to collect and analyze logs from various devices, helping to identify abnormal patterns and potential security incidents in the control plane. SIEM tools facilitate proactive monitoring and rapid response to security events, enhancing the overall security posture.

1.3.5 Compliance and regulation

Adhering to security standards and regulatory requirements is essential for organizations, especially in industries where data privacy and security are paramount. Control plane security measures contribute to meeting compliance standards by safeguarding critical network infrastructure and ensuring the confidentiality and integrity of sensitive information.

1.3.6 Minimizing the attack surface and zero trust architecture

By securing the control plane, organizations reduce the attack surface available to potential adversaries. This minimization helps protect against various cyber threats and enhances overall network resilience. Adopting a zero trust security model involves assuming that no entity, whether inside or outside the network, is trustworthy by default. This approach emphasizes the need for continuous authentication and authorization. Implementing zero trust principles in the control plane ensures that only authenticated and authorized entities can access critical network functions.

1.3.7 Quick detection and response

Implementing monitoring and alerting systems for the control plane allows organizations to quickly detect anomalous behavior or potential security incidents. Rapid response to security events in the control plane can help mitigate the impact of attacks and limit the extent of potential damage.

1.3.8 Secure routing protocols and regular security audits

Routing protocols are fundamental to the operation of the control plane. Securing these protocols involves implementing measures such as using authentication mechanisms (e.g., routing protocol authentication, RPKI) to verify the legitimacy of routing updates. Regularly auditing and monitoring routing information helps detect and mitigate route hijacking or manipulation attempts.

Conducting regular security audits of the control plane is essential for identifying and addressing vulnerabilities. Penetration testing and vulnerability assessments can uncover weaknesses that may be exploited by malicious actors. Periodic security reviews help ensure that control plane security measures are up-to-date and aligned with evolving cybersecurity threats.

Control plane security is fundamental to maintaining a robust and resilient network infrastructure. By implementing comprehensive security measures, organizations can safeguard the control plane from unauthorized access, prevent disruptions, and ensure the stability and reliability of their networks in the face of evolving cybersecurity threats. Control plane security is a multifaceted approach that involves a combination of technical measures, secure protocols, monitoring tools, and organizational practices. By addressing these aspects comprehensively, organizations can establish a resilient control plane that is capable of withstanding various cyber threats and maintaining the integrity and stability of their networks.

A secure communication line is employed to interact with the controller, significantly enhancing the controller's resistance to unauthorized access. In the context of basic software-defined networking (SDN) operations, potential attackers may exploit the new packet mechanism to disrupt communication with the controller. The inherent limitation on the size of flow tables in both the controller and network devices, attributable to memory constraints, poses a vulnerability. Attackers capitalize on this by inundating the network with packets bearing fake addresses, leading these packets to be routed to the controller. The heightened influx of packets can overwhelm the controller, monopolizing its resources for processing malicious packets (Haque et al., 2020).

A sustained influx of high-rate malicious packets has the potential to entirely incapacitate the controller, obstructing its accessibility to legitimate traffic. Such an onslaught may culminate in the collapse of the SDN architecture. Notably, the execution of this type of attack requires a considerable amount of time to accumulate a critical mass of malicious packets. Malicious actors employing a distributed denial of service (DDoS) strategy may orchestrate periodic attacks, strategically timing them to elude detection methods, thereby extending the window before their target is reached (Glvan et al., 2019).

In recent years, SDN security has emerged as a prominent and extensively discussed topic. SDN faces two significant security challenges: addressing conventional network security issues and fortifying the security of SDN-enabled infrastructure. The latter introduces seven key threat vectors that SDN is susceptible to. Among these vulnerabilities, a distributed denial of service (DDoS) attack on controllers stands out as the most devastating, posing a severe threat to the entire network. Efforts to secure SDN involve strategies aimed at both mitigating traditional security concerns and reinforcing the resilience of SDN-enabled infrastructures. Control plane security is a multifaceted approach that involves a combination of technical measures, secure protocols, monitoring tools, and organizational practices. By addressing these aspects comprehensively, organizations can establish a resilient control plane that is capable of withstanding various cyber threats and maintaining the integrity and stability of their networks.

Figure 1.5: DDoS attack on SDN using a botnet (Haque et al., 2018).

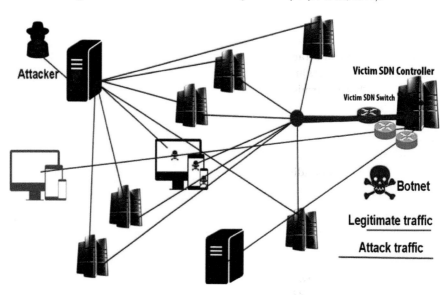

The controller's centralized nature makes it vulnerable to flood attacks, which can disrupt service across the entire network (Deepa et al., 2019). The impact of DDoS attacks on SDN networks is one of the most critical challenges. A DDoS attack on the SDN controller could deplete its processing resources, rendering it inaccessible to legitimate packets, affecting service availability (Thomas and James, 2017). When compared to traditional networks, DDoS attacks will be more effective and cause more damage in SDN networks (Mousavi and St-Hilaire, 2018). There are currently several research works that propose various methods of detecting and mitigating DDoS attacks in SDN environments, but there is no methodology that serves as a guide for the implementation of these solutions. DDoS aims to deplete the victim's resources by preventing legitimate users from accessing resources, causing financial and reputational harm. Although SDN is a promising solution and the future of networks, it is vulnerable to DDoS attacks.

DDoS attacks, as the name implies, are distributed in nature and can be launched across the globe by distributed botnets. The distributed nature of the attack, the variable duration pattern of the attack, the variety in the volume of the attack, the use of spoofed IP addresses, and the difficulty in identifying the traffic features are some of the main reasons why DDoS is difficult to detect and address (Jose et al., 2021). DoS can affect both the switches and the controllers in an SDN scenario. The switches in SDN are simple forwarding devices that forward packets based on the rules in the flow tables that the controller inserts. When a switch receives a packet, it compares it to the matching rule in its flow table and decides whether to perform the action defined for that rule. Figure 1.5 depicts an attacker sending a botnet to multiple devices all around the world. Usually, users are unaware that their devices have been infected with a botnet. The botnet armies will then receive a command from the attacker to attack at predetermined times and generate massive amounts of traffic to the victim's SDN application layer, data layer, and control layer server or service. As a result, the legitimate user's service will be disrupted. Because of modern-day telecommunication network interconnectivity, the magnitude and frequency of DDoS attacks are astounding. Aggressors use botnets to spread quickly.

References

[1] Anthony, L. (2015). Security Risks in SDN and Other New Software Issues. RSA Conference. Frost and Sullivan,

[2] Bannour, F., Souihi, S., & Mellouk, A. (2017). Distributed SDN control: Survey, taxonomy, and challenges. IEEE Communications Surveys & Tutorials, 20(1), 333-354.

[3] Deepa, V., Sudar, K. M., & Deepalakshmi, P. (2019). Design of ensemble learning methods for DDoS detection in SDN environment. 2019 International Conference on Vision Towards Emerging Trends in Communication and Networking (ViTECoN),

[4] Glvan, D., Rcuciu, C., Moinescu, R., & Antonie, N.-F. (2019). Detecting the DDoS attack for SDN Controller. Scientific Bulletin" Mircea cel Batran" Naval Academy, 22(1), 1-8.

[5] Hadi, F., Imran, M., Durad, M. H., & Waris, M. (2018). A simple security policy enforcement system for an institution using SDN controller. 2018 15th International Bhurban Conference on Applied Sciences and Technology (IBCAST),

[6] Haque, M. R., Tan, S. C., Lee, C. K., Yusoff, Z., Ali, S., Kaspin, I., & Ziri, S. R. (2018). Analysis of DDoS attack-aware software-defined networking controller placement in Malaysia. In Recent Trends in Computer Applications (pp. 175-188). Springer.

[7] Jose, A. S., Nair, L. R., & Paul, V. (2021). Towards Detecting Flooding DDOS Attacks Over Software Defined Networks Using Machine Learning Techniques. REVISTA GEINTEC-GESTAO INOVACAO E TECNOLOGIAS, 11(4), 3837-3865.

[8] Kalkan, K., & Zeadally, S. (2017). Securing internet of things with software defined networking. IEEE Communications Magazine, 56(9), 186-192.

[9]   Kandoi, R., & Antikainen, M. (2015). Denial-of-service attacks in OpenFlow SDN networks. 2015 IFIP/IEEE International Symposium on Integrated Network Management (IM),

[10] Kodzai, C. (2020). Impact of network security on SDN controller performance University of Cape Town.

[11] Kreutz, D., Ramos, F. M., Verissimo, P. E., Rothenberg, C. E., Azodolmolky, S., & Uhlig, S. (2014). Software-defined networking: A comprehensive survey. Proceedings of the IEEE, 103(1), 14-76.

[12] Lawal, B. H., & Nuray, A. (2018). Real-time detection and mitigation of distributed denial of service (DDoS) attacks in software defined networking (SDN). 2018 26th Signal Processing and Communications Applications Conference (SIU),

[13] Mladenov, B. (2019). Studying the DDoS attack effect over SDN controller southbound channel. 2019 X National Conference with International Participation (ELECTRONICA),

[14] Mousavi, S. M., & St-Hilaire, M. (2018). Early detection of DDoS attacks against software defined network controllers. Journal of Network and Systems Management, 26(3), 573-591.

[15] Salman, O., Elhajj, I. H., Kayssi, A., & Chehab, A. (2016). SDN controllers: A comparative study. 2016 18th mediterranean electrotechnical conference (MELECON).

[16] Stallings, W. (2015). Foundations of modern networking: SDN, NFV, QoE, IoT, and Cloud. Addison-Wesley Professional.

[17] Thomas, R. M., & James, D. (2017). DDOS detection and denial using third party application in SDN. 2017 International Conference on Energy, Communication, Data Analytics and Soft Computing (ICECDS).

[18] Z. Latif, K. Sharif, F. Li, M.M. Karim, S. Biswas, Y. Wang A comprehensive survey of interface protocols for software defined networks J. Netw. Comput. Appl., 156 (2020), Article 102563

CHAPTER

2

Understanding DDoS Attacks

This chapter explains the basics of distributed denial of service (DDoS) attacks within the software-defined networking (SDN). It starts by dissecting the core nature of these attacks, exposing their mechanisms and potential to cripple your network's operations. By understanding their inner workings, you gain the crucial advantage needed to develop effective defense strategies. Next, we embark on a historical journey, tracing the fascinating evolution of DDoS attacks over time. Witnessing their changing nature provides valuable insights into the motivations behind them and the ever-sophisticating tactics employed by attackers. This historical context equips you to anticipate future threats and adapt your defenses accordingly. Finally, we bridge the gap between theory and practice, exploring the specific ways in which DDoS attacks, a major security concern, directly impact SDN architectures. This crucial understanding empowers you to identify vulnerabilities within your SDN environment and implement targeted security measures to mitigate the risks. Whether you're a security professional, network administrator, or simply curious about the future of network security, this chapter offers valuable insights into this critical challenge in the world of SDN.

2.1 The Nature of DDoS Attacks

A distributed denial of service (DDoS) attack is a malicious attempt to disrupt the normal functioning of a targeted server, service, or network by overwhelming it with a flood of internet traffic. The term "distributed" implies that these attacks typically involve multiple sources, making it challenging to mitigate or defend against them effectively.

Here are key aspects that characterize the nature of DDoS attacks:

1. Distributed source:

   - DDoS attacks involve a large number of compromised computers, often referred to as a botnet. These compromised machines may be spread across the globe and controlled by a single entity or a group of attackers.
   - The distributed nature makes it difficult to trace and mitigate the attack since the traffic comes from multiple IP addresses.

2. Traffic volume:

   - DDoS attacks aim to flood the target with a massive amount of traffic, overwhelming its capacity to handle legitimate requests.
   - High-volume attacks can saturate the target's network bandwidth, making it difficult for legitimate users to access the targeted service.

3. Variety of attack vectors:

   - DDoS attacks can take various forms, each exploiting different vulnerabilities in the target's infrastructure.
   - Common attack vectors include:

     - Volumetric attacks: Flooding the target with a high volume of traffic.
     - Protocol attacks: Exploiting weaknesses in network protocols.
     - Application layer attacks: Targeting specific applications or services to exhaust resources.

4. Botnets:

   - Attackers often create botnets by infecting a large number of computers with malware. These compromised machines, known as bots, are then used to launch coordinated DDoS attacks.
   - The use of botnets provides attackers with significant resources and amplifies the impact of the attack.

5. Motivations:

- DDoS attacks can have various motivations, including financial gain, ideological reasons, revenge, or simply to cause disruption.
- Attackers may demand ransom from the target to stop the attack, or they may use DDoS as a distraction while carrying out other malicious activities.

6. Mitigation and defense:

- Mitigating DDoS attacks involves a combination of network infrastructure upgrades, traffic filtering, and the use of specialized DDoS mitigation services.
- Content delivery networks (CDNs) and DDoS mitigation providers can help absorb and filter malicious traffic, allowing only legitimate requests to reach the target.

The DDoS attack has emerged as a significant threat to cyberspace, as shown in the Figure 2.1. Understanding the nature of DDoS attacks is crucial for organizations to implement effective security measures and mitigate the impact of such attacks on their online services. Regular monitoring, incident response planning, and collaboration with DDoS mitigation services are essential components of a comprehensive defense strategy. DDoS attacks pose a significant threat to the availability and integrity of online services. Organizations must adopt a multi-faceted approach, combining infrastructure improvements, real-time monitoring, and collaboration with DDoS mitigation services to effectively defend against these attacks. Regular security audits and incident response drills are crucial components of a proactive defense strategy.

Figure 2.1: Growth in network-layer DDoS threat report for 2023 Q4 as seen by Cloudflare.

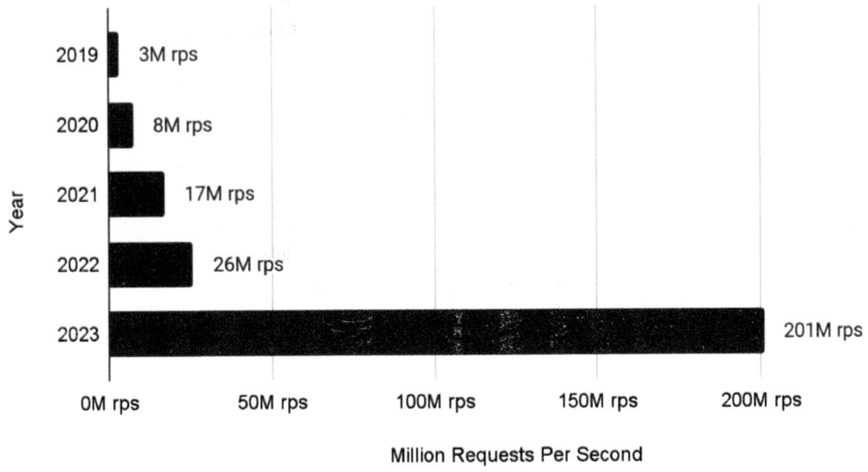

2.2 Historical Perspective and Evolution of DDoS Attacks

The history of distributed denial of service (DDoS) attacks dates back to the early days of the internet, with the evolution of these attacks reflecting the changing landscape of technology and cyber threats.

Here's a historical perspective on the development and evolution of DDoS attacks:

1. Late 1990s: Emergence of DDoS attacks:

    - The concept of DDoS attacks gained prominence in the late 1990s when attackers began using multiple systems to flood the network or overwhelm servers. These attacks were often carried out by script kiddies and hacktivist groups as a means of protest or online disruption.

2. Early attack tools:

    - In the late 1990s and early 2000s, simple attack tools like Trinoo, TFN (Tribe Flood Network), and Stacheldraht were developed to coordinate DDoS attacks. These tools allowed attackers to control multiple compromised systems and launch coordinated attacks.

3. 2000: "Mafiaboy" and the Yahoo! attack:

    - One of the early high-profile DDoS attacks occurred in 2000 when a teenager known as "Mafiaboy" launched a series of attacks targeting major websites, including Yahoo!, eBay, and CNN. This incident highlighted the vulnerability of even well-established online platforms to DDoS attacks.

4. 2007: Estonia cyberattacks:

    - In 2007, Estonia experienced a series of DDoS attacks that targeted government websites, banks, and media outlets. These attacks were believed to be politically motivated, as Estonia was involved in a diplomatic dispute with Russia at the time. The incident underscored the potential geopolitical impact of DDoS attacks.

5. 2010s: Rise of large-scale attacks:

- The 2010s saw a significant increase in the scale and complexity of DDoS attacks. Hacktivist groups like Anonymous gained attention for launching DDoS attacks as a form of online protest, targeting organizations perceived as adversaries.

6. Mirai botnet (2016):

- One of the most notorious events in DDoS history occurred in 2016 with the emergence of the Mirai botnet. Mirai targeted Internet of Things (IoT) devices, recruiting them into a massive botnet used to launch unprecedentedly large DDoS attacks. Mirai showcased the potential of compromising connected devices to amplify attack traffic.

7. 2018: Memcached reflection attacks:

- In 2018, attackers exploited misconfigured Memcached servers to launch powerful reflection/amplification attacks. These attacks demonstrated how attackers could leverage legitimate services to generate massive volumes of traffic directed at their targets.

8. Current trends (2020s):

   (a) DDoS attacks continue to evolve in the 2020s, with attackers leveraging increasingly sophisticated techniques, including DNS amplification, protocol-level exploits, and application layer attacks. The use of artificial intelligence and machine learning by both attackers and defenders has introduced a new dimension to the arms race in DDoS mitigation.

9. DDoS-for-hire services and ransom attacks:

- The proliferation of DDoS-for-hire services, often known as "booter" or "stresser" services, has made it easier for individuals with little technical expertise to launch DDoS attacks for various purposes. Additionally, some attackers use DDoS attacks as a distraction or part of a larger extortion scheme, demanding ransom payments to stop the attacks.

10. Legislation and international cooperation:

- Governments and law enforcement agencies worldwide have recognized the seriousness of DDoS attacks. Some countries have enacted legislation to address DDoS offenses, and international cooperation is often required to investigate and prosecute those responsible for large-scale attacks.

The historical evolution of DDoS attacks reflects the ongoing cat-and-mouse game between attackers and defenders. As technology advances, DDoS mitigation strategies must also evolve to address new attack vectors and protect the increasingly interconnected digital landscape.

Here are some of the key developments and trends in the historical evolution of DDoS attacks:

1. Increasing scale and complexity:

   - Over the years, the scale of DDoS attacks has grown significantly. While early attacks involved relatively small numbers of compromised systems, modern DDoS attacks can harness massive botnets comprising thousands or even millions of devices. The complexity of these attacks has also increased, incorporating various techniques to bypass traditional mitigation measures.

2. Amplification techniques:

   - Attackers have continually refined amplification techniques to increase the volume of attack traffic. DNS amplification, NTP amplification, and SNMP amplification attacks involve exploiting poorly configured servers to generate large amounts of traffic directed at the target. These techniques significantly amplify the impact of DDoS attacks.

3. IoT-based DDoS attacks:

   - The Mirai botnet in 2016 marked a turning point by exploiting insecure IoT devices to create a massive botnet. Since then, the trend of leveraging vulnerable IoT devices for DDoS attacks has continued. IoT devices often have weak security measures, making them attractive targets for inclusion in botnets.

4. Reflection and resilience:

   - Reflection attacks, where attackers use third-party servers to amplify and reflect attack traffic, have become more prevalent. Simultaneously, defenders have improved their resilience against DDoS attacks by implementing more robust and scalable infrastructures, often utilizing cloud-based DDoS protection services.

5. Application layer attacks:

- While volumetric attacks remain common, there is an increasing focus on application layer attacks. These attacks target specific vulnerabilities in web applications, APIs, or other services, aiming to exhaust server resources or disrupt the functionality of the targeted application. Examples include HTTP floods, Slowloris, and SQL injection attacks.

6. DDoS as a distraction:

- In some cases, DDoS attacks are used as a diversionary tactic. Cybercriminals launch a DDoS attack to draw attention and resources away from other malicious activities, such as data exfiltration or unauthorized access. This makes it challenging for defenders to prioritize and respond effectively.

7. Machine learning and AI in DDoS defense:

- Both attackers and defenders have started incorporating machine learning and artificial intelligence into their strategies. Attackers may use AI to enhance the effectiveness of their attacks, while defenders leverage these technologies to analyze network traffic patterns, identify anomalies, and automate the response to DDoS incidents in real-time.

8. Regulatory responses:

- Recognizing the serious impact of DDoS attacks, some countries have introduced or updated legislation specifically addressing cybercrimes, including DDoS offenses. Regulatory frameworks aim to hold individuals or groups accountable for launching such attacks and facilitate international cooperation in prosecuting offenders.

9. Shift towards ransom-based attacks:

- In addition to traditional motivations such as activism or revenge, some DDoS attacks now have a financial motivation. Attackers may launch DDoS attacks and demand a ransom payment to cease the attack. This type of extortion has become a significant concern for businesses that rely on online services.

10. Hybrid and multi-vector attacks:

- To overcome defense mechanisms, attackers increasingly employ hybrid and multi-vector attacks. These involve combining different attack vectors in a single campaign, making it more challenging for defenders to mitigate the attacks effectively. Hybrid attacks may include a combination of volumetric, protocol, and application layer attack methods.

The ongoing evolution of DDoS attacks underscores the need for a dynamic and adaptive approach to cybersecurity. Organizations must continually update their defense strategies, leverage emerging technologies, and collaborate with cybersecurity experts to stay ahead of evolving threats in the ever-changing landscape of cyber warfare.

2.3 DDoS Attack Vectors and their Impact on SDNs

The DDoS attack is a multi-computer-directed attack that uses "bots" or "zombies," which are networks of computers that are remotely controlled by an attacker to launch massive attacks on a specific target (Sahoo et al., 2017). Its motivation is to deplete network resources so that the service is hampered or stopped, resulting in a lack of service availability. A large number of packets are sent to one or more hosts on the network during the attack. If the source IP addresses of incoming packets are spoofed (which is common), the switch will not find a match in its flow table and will have to forward the packet to the controller. The accumulation of legitimate user packets and attacker-generated packets can adversely impact the SDN controller's available resources for communication, calculation, and storage, potentially exhausting them completely in the worst-case scenario. Even if there is a backup controller, it must deal with the same problem.

DDoS attacks can be held out on all three planes of the SDN architecture. DDoS attacks are classified into three types based on their potential targets: application-layer DDoS attacks, control layer DDoS attacks, and data layer DDoS attacks. Whatever the target, all of these attacks share the trait of flooding the network with massive amounts of packets, typically internet control message protocol (ICMP), transmission control protocol (TCP), or packets user datagram protocol (UDP). DDoS is essentially a flood attack. Many packets are sent to a network device to stop the service or reduce the device's performance. If the incoming source addresses are spoofed, the switch will not find a match and the packet will be forwarded to the controller. The accumulation of DDoS spoofed packets and legitimate packets can force the controller into continuous processing, exhausting them. As a result, the controller is no longer reachable for new legitimate packets. This will bring the controller down, causing the

SDN architecture to mess up. The same problem exists for a backup controller. Such attacks can be detected early on by monitoring a few hundred packets and looking for changes in entropy.

The early detection of DDoS attacks prevents the controller from being taken offline. The term "early" refers to the controller's tolerance level and the amount of traffic handled. As a result, the impact of malicious packet flooding can be mitigated. A portable machine with a fast response time is required. The fast response time allows the controller to regain control by terminating the DDoS attack during the attack period (Cui et al., 2021). The control plane is one of the most appealing targets for DoS and DDoS attacks. Because network resources are visible, the SDN controller can become a single point of failure, exposing the entire network to a security attack.

Distributed denial of service (DDoS) attacks target the availability and functionality of online services by overwhelming a target with a flood of malicious traffic. The impact of DDoS attacks is particularly significant in software-defined networking (SDN) environments, where the network architecture is programmable and centrally managed. Here, we'll explore various DDoS attack vectors and their specific impact on SDN:

1. Volumetric attacks:

    - **Impact on SDN:** Volumetric attacks flood the network with a high volume of traffic, consuming bandwidth and causing congestion. In SDN, this can lead to a saturation of the network links, disrupting the flow of legitimate traffic and impacting the overall performance of the SDN infrastructure.

2. Protocol attacks:

    - **Impact on SDN:** Protocol-based attacks exploit vulnerabilities in network protocols, consuming resources on SDN controllers and switches. This can result in increased latency, degraded network performance, and potential disruption of communication between SDN components.

3. Application layer attacks:

    - **Impact on SDN:** Application layer attacks target specific applications or services, overwhelming their resources. In SDN, attacks against application layer services can lead to the exhaustion of controller resources, affecting the management and control plane functionality. This may result in delayed or failed responses to network events.

4.   Reflection and amplification attacks:

- **Impact on SDN:** Reflection attacks, which use third-party servers to amplify and reflect attack traffic, can overwhelm SDN controllers and switches. The amplification factor can strain the computational capabilities of SDN components, affecting their ability to manage network policies and traffic flow.

5.   SYN/ACK floods:

- **Impact on SDN:** SYN/ACK floods exploit the TCP handshake process, overwhelming the target with connection requests. In SDN, this can lead to the exhaustion of available connection resources on switches and controllers, disrupting the establishment of new flows and impacting network responsiveness.

6.   DNS amplification:

- **Impact on SDN:** DNS amplification attacks leverage misconfigured DNS servers to amplify attack traffic. In SDN, these attacks can saturate the network with DNS response packets, affecting the availability and performance of DNS services utilized by the SDN infrastructure.

7.   NTP amplification:

- **Impact on SDN:** Network time protocol (NTP) amplification attacks exploit misconfigured NTP servers to amplify attack traffic. In SDN, this can lead to increased latency and resource consumption on SDN controllers, impacting the synchronization and coordination of network policies.

8.   IoT-based DDoS attacks:

- **Impact on SDN:** DDoS attacks leveraging compromised IoT devices can generate a massive volume of traffic directed at SDN components. The sheer scale of these attacks can overwhelm SDN controllers and switches, affecting their ability to manage network resources and enforce policies.

9.   Application-layer protocols exploitation:

- **Impact on SDN:** Attackers may exploit vulnerabilities in application-layer protocols used in SDN, such as OpenFlow. Exploits targeting these protocols can disrupt the communication between SDN controllers and switches, leading to a breakdown in the centralized control and orchestration of network resources.

10.   Slowloris attacks:

- **Impact on SDN:** Slowloris attacks attempt to exhaust server resources by keeping numerous connections open simultaneously. In SDN, these attacks can target controller resources, causing delays in processing and responding to network events, and potentially leading to service disruptions.

11.   DNS spoofing and cache poisoning:

- **Impact on SDN:** DNS spoofing and cache poisoning attacks can disrupt DNS resolution within SDN environments, affecting the ability of controllers to accurately resolve domain names. Compromised DNS information can lead to misdirected traffic, causing confusion in the network and potentially enabling further attacks.

12.   Zero-day exploits and SDN controllers:

- **Impact on SDN:** Zero-day exploits targeting vulnerabilities in SDN controllers can have severe consequences. If attackers discover and exploit unknown vulnerabilities, they may gain unauthorized access to the controller, compromising the centralized management of the network and potentially causing widespread disruption.

13.   SDN southbound link saturation:

- **Impact on SDN:** Attackers may target the southbound links between SDN controllers and switches to saturate communication channels. This can disrupt the flow of control messages, impacting the ability of controllers to enforce policies and manage network resources effectively.

14.   Resource exhaustion attacks:

- **Impact on SDN:** DDoS attacks that aim to exhaust the computational resources of SDN controllers can disrupt the orchestration and coordination of network policies. Resource exhaustion can result in delayed response times, rendering the SDN infrastructure less capable of adapting to dynamic changes in network conditions.

15.   Load balancer exploitation:

- **Impact on SDN:** Load balancers play a crucial role in distributing traffic efficiently in SDN environments. Attackers may exploit vulnerabilities in load balancing mechanisms, causing uneven distribution or failure in load balancing. This can lead to congestion on certain network paths and impact overall network performance.

16. SDN application layer attacks:

- **Impact on SDN:** SDN applications, which provide additional functionality and services, can become targets of application layer attacks. Compromising SDN applications may lead to disruptions in specific services or functionalities, affecting the overall performance and reliability of the SDN environment.

17. SDN controller spoofing:

- **Impact on SDN:** Spoofing attacks that impersonate SDN controllers can disrupt the proper functioning of the network. By injecting malicious control messages into the network, attackers can manipulate traffic flows, compromise security policies, and potentially cause unauthorized access to network resources.

18. Packet fragmentation attacks:

- **Impact on SDN:** Fragmented packets can be used in DDoS attacks to exploit vulnerabilities in packet reassembly processes. In SDN, attacks leveraging packet fragmentation can disrupt the normal functioning of switches and controllers, leading to processing delays and potential service disruptions.

19. SDN flow table exhaustion:

- **Impact on SDN:** Attackers may attempt to exhaust the flow table capacity of SDN switches by overwhelming them with a high rate of flow creation requests. This can disrupt the ability of switches to efficiently process and forward network traffic, causing performance degradation and potential denial of service.

20. Machine learning evasion:

- **Impact on SDN:** Some advanced DDoS attacks may employ machine learning evasion techniques to bypass traditional detection mechanisms. In SDN, attackers could leverage these evasion techniques to deceive security algorithms and avoid timely identification, allowing the attack to persist for longer durations.

Mitigating the impact of DDoS attacks on SDNs involves implementing robust security measures, including traffic filtering, rate limiting, and the use of DDoS mitigation services. Additionally, SDN architectures can benefit from adaptive security mechanisms that dynamically adjust to evolving threats and anomalous network behavior. Mitigating these diverse and evolving threats to SDNs requires a combination of proactive security measures. This includes the implementation of intrusion detection and prevention systems, regular security audits, anomaly detection, and the integration of adaptive security solutions that can dynamically adjust to emerging threats. The collaboration between network security professionals and SDN architects is crucial to developing resilient and secure SDN infrastructures.

References

[1]   Cui, Y., Qian, Q., Guo, C., Shen, G., Tian, Y., Xing, H., & Yan, L. (2021). Towards DDoS detection mechanisms in software-defined networking. Journal of Network and computer Applications, 103156.

[2]   Sahoo, K. S., Sarkar, A., Mishra, S. K., Sahoo, B., Puthal, D., Obaidat, M. S., & Sadun, B. (2017). Metaheuristic solutions for solving controller placement problem in SDN-based WAN architecture. ICETE 2017-Proceedings of the 14th International Joint Conference on e-Business and Telecommunications,

3

Proposed Detection Methodology

Cybersecurity is paramount in the dynamic world of software-defined networks (SDNs), where ever-evolving threats demand proactive and intelligent defense mechanisms. This chapter unveils a cutting-edge detection system designed to safeguard your SDN environment, offering a comprehensive analysis of its design principles and practical implementation. First, we explore the foundational design principles that underpin its effectiveness. These principles guide the system's architecture, ensuring adaptability, scalability, and efficient resource utilization within the unique context of SDNs. Through understanding these guiding principles, you gain insight into the system's inherent strengths and its suitability for your specific security needs.

Next, we unveil the intricate mechanisms powering the detection engine. The chapter dives deep into the algorithmic approach employed, highlighting the specific algorithms chosen and their role in identifying suspicious activity. Additionally, we explore the system's data analysis techniques, showcasing how it effectively leverages the wealth of data available within an SDN environment to uncover hidden patterns and anomalies indicative of potential threats. By understanding these core functionalities, you gain confidence in the system's ability to accurately detect even the most sophisticated attacks. Finally, the chapter bridges the gap between theory and practice. We demonstrate the practical application of the proposed detection system by showcasing its integration with SDN controllers. This seamless integration ensures that security measures remain agile and adapt to the dynamic nature of SDN environments, guaranteeing real-time threat detection and swift response capabilities. Witnessing this integration provides valuable insights into how the system can be deployed within your own network infrastructure for comprehensive protection.

3.1 Designing the Detection System

The purpose of this book is to construct a methodology for integrating a mechanism for detecting and monitoring DDoS attacks on the SDN control plane. As a promising technology, the SDN and its associated security issues lack the necessary methodological proposals for implementation. The standard's structure will be based on the outlined mandatory sections, which are also consistent with the series of steps. The application of these internationally recognized standards ensures a complete and orderly methodology that can be used in any type of organization. The methodology will be developed by first identifying the risks and technical vulnerabilities of the SDN controller and then establishing an adequate solution based on the requirements demanded by the solution. The proposed solution will be tested in a controlled simulation environment to collect data, identify and correct flaws in the methodology, and finally validate it.

As a result of the implementation of this methodology, a guide for detecting and mitigating this type of security impact will be obtained as shown in Figure 3.1. It will be a guide that, when followed precisely, will assist professionals in technological areas, particularly information security, in improving the security of the SDN control plane, which is the most critical point in this type of architecture.

During a DDoS attack, a high number of packets are sent to a host or a group of hosts on a network. If the source addresses of arriving packets are forged, as is usual, the switch will not detect a match and will have to pass the packet to the controller. By forcing the controller's resources into continuous processing, the accumulation of valid and DDoS faked packets might exhaust them. This renders the controller unavailable for freshly incoming legal packets and may result in the controller failing, resulting in the SDN architecture's weakening. As a result, a quick and effective method of mitigating the attack is required. The randomness of incoming packets is measured here. Entropy, which is used to detect DDoS attacks, is a good measure of randomness.

Figure 3.1: System design components.

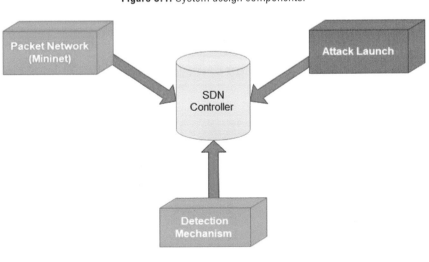

The aim of the study is to inspire and build an entropy-based technique for packet generation and detection of DDoS flood attacks in SDNs, as well as to mitigate DDoS attacks on the SDN controller. To be successful with this implementation, we must examine the requirements for deploying a secure controller as well as the benchmark performance KPIs for normal SDN network operation. We see that security design considerations for SDN-based architectures continue to be critical in the evolution of SDN technology due to security vulnerabilities introduced by centralizing control logic. This will inevitably necessitate a great deal of attention in order to provide stability to the new SDN solution. Hackers continue to target the SDN controller, which necessitates a strong defense against external networks and software-based intrusions.

This chapter will outline the proposed approach for early detection. Due to the controller's limited resources, the attack should be detected within the first few hundred packets. The formulae for entropy, the experimental network topology, and the implementation setups needed for security solutions and computation will be covered. The proposed detection method will then be examined, followed by an assessment of early detection. This section additionally explains how to cope with the challenges mentioned in this book by implementing and adhering to the proposed model architecture shown in Figure 3.2.

Figure 3.2: Proposed model architecture.

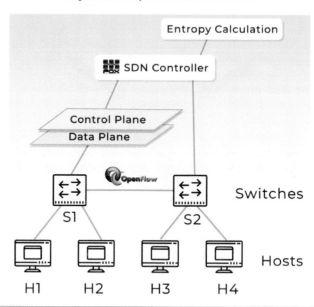

3.2 Algorithmic Approach and Data Analysis

In the previous section, we looked at the main components of entropy and how it can be used to detect DDoS. By looking at the formulation and computation in this section. This method examines the level of randomness in the traffic arriving at the controller (each host has an average number of packets it attempts to reach per unit of time). Entropy is a critical concept in information theory. The ability of entropy to measure randomness in a network is the primary reason for using it. The greater the randomness, the greater the entropy, and vice versa. DDoS detection using entropy requires two components: window size and a threshold.

The size of the window is set by either time or a series of packets. Entropy is calculated inside this timeframe to estimate the uncertainty in the arriving packets. An assault must be detected by a threshold. Depending on the technique, an attack is detected when the estimated entropy exceeds or falls below a threshold. If n is the number of packets in a window and p_i is the probability of each element in the window, then the entropy (H) is calculated using the Shannon entropy formula of Equation (3.3). Any pattern will deviate from this rule and impose a particular order.

A pattern is identified by two factors: Window sizes and threshold. The window size, which is determined by a period or the number of packets per window, allows you to quantify incoming traffic. The target parameter is measured in the header field of each window. The threshold is equal to the minimum entropy value measured during normal traffic flow. Entropy is calculated within the window to determine the randomness of the following packets. When the entropy value falls below a certain threshold, it indicates that an attack is underway. Entropy is greatest when all elements have equal probabilities.

When one element appears more frequently than others, the entropy increases. If there is a steady stream of incoming data, it is divided into equal sets known as windows. Each element and its occurrence are counted in the window. When the entropy falls below a certain threshold, we can say that a DDoS attack has occurred. To identify an attack in the controller, check the destination IP address of incoming packets. The controller now contains a method for constructing an incoming packet hash table. When an IP address is entered into the database for the first time, it will be counted as one. If an instance of it exists in the table, its count will be increased. Let W be a data set with n elements and x be an event within the set.

$$W = [(x1, y1), (x2, y2), (x3, y3), \ldots .]$$ (3.1)

$$p_i = \frac{x_i}{n}$$ (3.2)

$$H = -\sum_{i=1}^{n} p_i \log p_i$$ (3.3)

The entropy of the window will be calculated after a certain packet. Equation (3.1) depicts the hash table, where x represents the destination IP address and y represents the number of times it appeared. We use Equations (3.1) and (3.2) to estimate the entropy shown in Equation (3.3), where W is the window and p_i is the probability of each IP address, and where x is the number of events in the set and n is the size of the window. We use two factors to calculate entropy for detection in this case: one is the destination IP address and another is the number of times it was repeated.

The entropy will be at its highest when each IP address only occurs once. A large number of packets will be directed to a host if an attack is directed at it. These packets will take up the majority of the window, lowering the number of distinct IP addresses in the window and, as a result, entropy. For new packets, entropy will be calculated based on the destination IP address. When there is an attack, the entropy decreases because the IP address of the host or hosts under attack appears more frequently. Because detection takes place within the controller, this work will be customized for the SDN environment.

3.2.1 What is the significance of entropy?

The source address is always new when packets arrive at the controller. This is why they seek the controller's assistance. Because there is no instance of them in the switch's table, they are passed on to the controller. For each new incoming connection, the controller will install a flow in the switch, routing the rest of the incoming packets to the destination without additional processing. As a result, every packet displayed in the controller is completely fresh.

Another known truth about newly arriving packets reaching the controller is that the destination host is in the controller's network. The network is comprised of the switches and hosts that connect to it. Given that the packet is fresh and its destination is within the network, the quantity of randomness may be defined by computing the entropy based on a window size. The window size is defined as the number of arriving new packets required to compute entropy. When each packet is meant for exactly one host, maximum entropy is achieved. When all packets in a window are bound for the same host, the entropy is at its lowest. SDN is an effective way of detecting DDoS because it can quantify randomness and have minimum and maximum values based on entropy. Whenever a large number of packets attack a single host or a subnet of hosts, the value of entropy can drop.

In the second chapter, we discovered that the two methods required extensive training to detect anomalies. In addition, intrusion detection devices for DDoS detection had to be installed on various network links. These limitations do not apply to entropy.

3.2.2 Window sizing

To provide accurate calculations, the window size should be less than or equal to the number of hosts. For this study, it was chosen a window packet of 50. The main reason for selecting 50 is that each host in the network has a limited number of incoming new connections. Once a connection is established in SDN, packets will not pass through the controller unless a new request is made. Additional reason is that each controller is limited to a certain number of switches and hosts. The computation performed for each window is the third reason for selecting this size.

A list of 50 values may be calculated significantly more quickly than a list of 500 values, and an attack can be detected much sooner in a 50-packet window. It is chosen to be 50 because the number of hosts in the test network is less than

100. It is also measured the CPU as well as memory usage tested the entropy with three different window sizes. The threshold is determined by the rate of normal traffic, which is traffic that is not classed as attack traffic. To address queries about the strength of the attack, a simple fraction of attack packets P_a to normal traffic packets P_n equals the rate R as shown in Equation (3.4).

$$R = (P_a \div P_n) \times 100\% \tag{3.4}$$

Running a lightweight application on the SDN controller helps detect DDoS attempts on a server in an SDN network. The program counts the number of packets flooding into the SDN controller, calculates the packet rate and data

Figure 3.3: DDoS detection and mitigation flowchart.

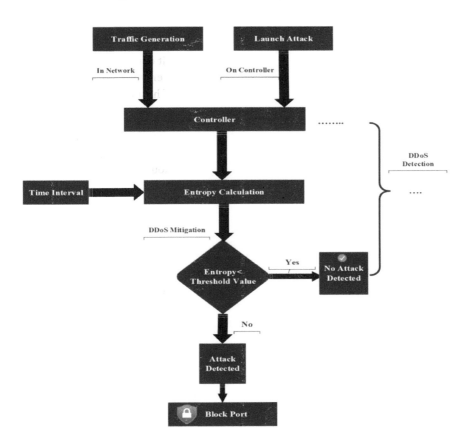

packet occurrences based on the destination IP address, TCP port, and source IP address, and determines the entropy of the destination IP address, TCP port, and source IP address 4 as depicted in the algorithm flow chart of Figure 3.3.

The quantitative approach was used to address the research problem. The quantitative data obtained from the simulation will be interpreted, and the proposed methodology will be validated.

3.3 Integration with SDN Controllers

This section describes and expands on the specifications and customization options for the tools that will be used in the experiments. The details will provide the reader with the requirements for the proof-of-concept implementation, as well as the method of setup and configuration that will be used to deliver the proposed solution. The proposed solution will be implemented on the Ubuntu platform using the POX controller. Under a set of specific conditions, the functional requirements define how the proposed solution will work, behave, and deliver a working model. It describes the proposed system features and capabilities of each component of the overall solution in terms of DDoS attack detection and mitigation functionality. The key points of functionality are listed below and these programs were used for this project mainly meanwhile setup details and feature requirements are listed in Appendices A1, A2, A3 and A4.

(a)   Virtual box: Provides a foundation for the formation of a virtual network.

(b)   Mininet: Feferred to as virtual SDN network topology.

(c)   POX: An SDN controller, as shown in the proposed model architecture of Figure 3.2.

The following hardware and software features were used in this experiment on an ASUS laptop. The experimental operating system is based on Ubuntu Linux and runs Ubuntu image files in Oracle VM VirtualBox software. Mininet's version is 2.3.0, and it runs locally on Linux in Appendix A3. The proposed technology is tested in a simulation environment to ensure its validity. The software to use is Mininet, a widely used tool for simulating SDN architectures. The program runs on an Ubuntu virtual machine with the VirtualBox virtualization software. However, within the software tools used in this project are

- Oracle VM VirtualBox
- Wireshark Packet Analyzer

- Python and VS code
- Secure CRT ® SSH and SFTP tool
- Mininet
- Microsoft Visio 2021
- XD 2022.

Here the most recent version of VirtualBox was used to host a virtual machine with the most recent version of Ubuntu, as this is what has been recommended for running the Mininet simulation software. The information about the virtual machine and its hardware specifications are available in Appendix A4.

The subsections below describes the tools and technologies used to build the test platforms used in the experiments. All of the tools used in the PoC are opensource Linux Ubuntu VirtualBox software. The specific software versions and integration interfaces for all of the tools are further explained, as is the build-up in delivery of a converged secure SDN platform.

3.3.1 Packet generation and manipulation in the Linux platform

Scapy is in charge of packet generation. It is an extremely effective tool for package generation, scanning, sniffing, attacking, and forgery. Scapy has two parameters such as packet type and packet generation interval. TCP and UDP packets are included in the packet type. UDP packets are used to forge packet source IP addresses. The interval is tailored to the test case. In this experiment, Scapy is used to generate network traffic in order to simulate both normal and attack traffic. With Scapy, forged IP packets can be generated, masking the identity of the true attacker. Run the Scapy program on the host to send packets to the host in the designed network topology, both normal and attack packets (UDP packets and TCP packets).

Scapy is a free and open-source program and is written in the Python programming language. Scapy is a program that manipulates packets, the Scapy tool forges data packets that come from a source, and Scapy decodes and captures data packets. This tool reads packets from pcap files and then compares them to the request and replies. The Scapy tool also performs scanning such as trace-routing and unit tests. You can also use the Scapy tool to perform Nmap scanning 2 .This tool is also very good at a variety of other tasks that most other tools cannot handle, such as sending invalid frames, VLAN hopping+ARP cache poisoning, and VoIP decoding on WEP-protected channels. Because this tool is written in Python, it supports Python 2.7 and Python 3.

(3.4 to 3.7). This is a multi- platform tool that is available for Windows, Linux OSX, and *BSD. The Scapy tool can be used as a shell to interact with network incoming and outgoing traffic 2.

3.3.2 POX

It is critical to select an appropriate controller. There are numerous controllers available for researchers and developers at the moment. As shown in Table 3.1, this book selects some representative controllers and compares their basic information. In this experiment, the POX controller is used. It is widely used in high speed, lightweight experiments. It is intended to be a platform upon which a user-defined controller can be built. POX is a Python-based opensource controller. Its advantage is that it simplifies the application interface to the controller, allowing it to run in parallel with the controller. Stanford developed the POX controller, which is based on OpenFlow. POX is made up of two parts: the kernel and the component. All components communicate with one another through the kernel, which serves as the assembly point for all components.

POX contains an OpenFlow interface for discovering topologies and selecting paths, as well as the ability to customize components to perform specific functions. POX controller enables rapid development of controller prototype functions and can generate superior performance applications, reducing developer burden and improving development efficiency. POX is a general-purpose SDN controller written in Python that supports OpenFlow.

Table 3.1: SDN controllers.

Controller	Language	OpenFlow	Thread	Released
Ryu	Python	1.0–1.4	Single	03/2015
POX	Python	1.0–2.3	Single	10/2013
Nox	C++	1.0 and 1.3	Multiple	02/2014
Beacon	Java	1.0	Multiple	09/2013
Floodlight	Java	1.0	Multiple	11/2012
Opendaylight	Java	1.0 and 1.3	/	03/2015
ONOS	Java	1.0 and 1.3	/	03/2015

It has a high-level SDN API with a representative topology graph and virtualization support.

The Python-based POX SDN controller will be used in the experimental setup for this dissertation because it is regarded as a suitable platform for the implementation of SDNs in the academic and research fields. POX is a simple and lightweight design on which several academic studies and prototypes of SDN projects have been carried out. POX has attracted the attention of many developers and researchers due to its advantages of programming language, clear architecture, good performance, and strong scalability, in addition to the advantages of programming language. For the reasons stated above, the POX controller was chosen for the simulation experiment in this work.

3.3.3 Mininet

Mininet, SDN-based network emulation software, is used in the PoC to simulate and create virtual hosts, SDN switches, and a reference controller. Mininet is a vital modeling tool for SDN-based networks that offers information on how the POX controller will react under preset security circumstances. Mininet will connect with the POX controller as a remote controller through a LAN virtual switch generated on the virtualization program VirtualBox, which is installed on an Ubuntu desktop OS virtual machine in the PoC. The external controller is referred to by a remote controller and its associated IP address. Mininet software was chosen because of its flexibility, scalability, and ability to be adjusted for any unique topologies and features 3. It also supports OpenFlow 1.0 or 1.3, an industry accepted standard with multi-vendor controller interoperability, which is essential for constructing SDN-based networks. The Mininet program was created in Python and offers a Python API for building bespoke networks depending on network simulation and prototype needs 1. To analyze the OpenFlow messages used in the connection setup, the software can be easily integrated with packet monitoring software such as Wireshark.

3.3.4 OpenFlow switches

OpenFlow switches are critical components of SDN-based networking because they provide data plane routing and traffic forwarding for hosts. The OpenFlow switches are simulated in the Mininet software and connect to the POX remote controller via the OpenFlow protocol. Flow or group tables in OpenFlow switches perform packet lookups and forward traffic based on reactive or preloaded flow actions for the traffic type in question. Installed traffic rules installed by interrogating the POX controller determine the OpenFlow switch forwarding actions. This happens if it comes across a table miss for no matching flows in the switch rules database. The OpenFlow switch sends a PACKET IN message to the controller when it receives a request. The PACKET IN message encapsulates the original host traffic or TCP packet header information, as well as a buffer ID for the stored packet for future reference. The controller will send a PACKET OUT message to the switch with handling instructions as a FLOW-MOD modification, which includes various actions to forward, flood, or drop the packet 3. By referencing the buffer IDs of previously installed actions in the flow tables, the OpenFlow switches can construct group tables with appropriate actions to all future packets using this advanced logic.

3.3.5 Oracle VM VirtualBox

VirtualBox is a virtualization tool that enables server or desktop virtualization as well as storage virtualization on the same physical machine. Oracle VM VirtualBox allows virtual machine software to execute directly on the host's CPU, but an array of sophisticated methods is utilized to intercept actions that would interfere with your host. Oracle VM VirtualBox intervenes and takes action when a visitor attempts to do something that might be detrimental to your machine or its data. Oracle VM VirtualBox, in particular, simulates a specific virtual environment based on how you built a virtual machine to access a huge quantity of hardware that the guest believes it is accessing When a visitor seeks to access a hard drive, Oracle VM VirtualBox sends the request to the virtual hard disk that you have configured for the virtual machine. This is often an image file on your host. The utility is capable of running different operating systems, including Linux and old Windows operating systems, allowing for easy testing and experimental trials of software development. The VirtualBox tool dynamically adjusts the allocated virtual machine resources, ensuring efficient use of the physical host machine. The tool also has no additional license requirements, making it superior to other virtualization tools.

3.3.6 Ubuntu 20.04.3 LTS

Ubuntu 20.04 is a free and open-source Linux distribution that may be installed on a desktop or a server. The operating system is easy to set up and allows the user to customize and install necessary packages based on their needs. Using the VirtualBox tool mentioned in Section 3.3.2 of the PoC, we will construct a

VM for the POX controller and install the Mininet packet forwarder network using Linux. The basic operating system for our programs is Debian Ubuntu version 20.04. This Linux kernel was chosen because it supports all of the SDN protocols as well as all of the software packages needed for the PoC. Ubuntu 20.04 includes support for the Python application (required by POX), the OpenFlow protocol (virtual switches), hosts (security solution), Mininet, and a variety of other opensource protocols. The Ubuntu software also has no licensing requirements and relatively good support, with documentation on the internet and Linux Debian-based forums, but most importantly, it offers long-term services.

3.3.7 Wireshark packet analyzer

Wireshark is a network protocol analysis tool that may be used in both real-time and offline mode. Wireshark is an opensource tool that runs on a variety of platforms, including Windows, macOS, Linux, and FreeBSD, and provides deep packet inspection and decryption capabilities on a variety of secure protocols, including UDP, TCP, ICMP, SNMPv3, and in the PoC implementation, DDoS communications between the POX controller and the VM generating the DDoS traffic will be analyzed using Wireshark. It is a highly valuable tool in traffic analysis since it can extract OpenFlow messages created between OpenFlow switches and the POX controller. Wireshark will collect all IP packets created by network interface cards, including WIFI, local area network cards, and virtual interfaces, while operating in the background. The Wireshark utility will employ filters to identify the suitable interface for traffic listening and the related parameters (IP address, protocol, or MAC address) of interest in order to extract relevant traffic while preserving disk space.

3.3.8 Mininet Python API and protocols

The Mininet module serves as the core software for the packet forwarding network simulations in the proof of concept. The simulations will be carried out by configuring and executing a Python-based script using the emulator software's built-in Python API. The PoC will build the packet forwarding networks using custom Python scripts, making it simple to customize parameters like topology OpenFlow version, remote controller IP address, and OpenFlow port for connection to the POX controller. Due to the various permutations in the various test cases, the custom network option will provide easy deployment, scalability, and easy modifications to network configurations.

The southbound protocol that allows communication between the OVS switches and the POX controller is OpenFlow 3. OpenFlow enables controller to controller communication by utilizing the OpenFlow channel established between the switch and the controller. OpenFlow is required in the PoC for SDN network setup to POX controller through the use of the entropy calculation hash table. The Open V switch database (OVSDB) is a programmable switch management protocol that is used in SDN network deployments 3. In the experiments, the OVSDB is used in the data forwarding network mostly through OpenFlow.

3.3.9 Methodological framework

This section explains how to find solutions to the problems raised by the work. The study area is a controlled simulation environment in which an SDN will be implemented. The Mininet tool will be used to run the tests because it is the industry standard for SDN network virtualization. First, it is able to create a Mininet topology with 9 switches and 64 hosts, as proven within the Figure 3.4.

Figure 3.4: Proposed logical network topology.

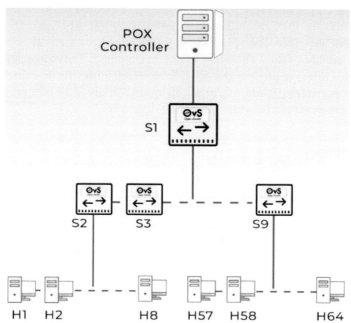

A network is attached to an OpenFlow controller. The entropy of visitors associated with the controller is then measured under regular and attack situations. Because it runs on Python, we used the POX controller for this challenge. A Mininet is a network emulator used to create network topology. Packet technology is achieved with the help of Wireshark, in which Wireshark is used for packet generation, sniffing, scanning, packet forging, and attacking. Wireshark is used to generate UDP packets and spoof the packets' source IP address.

References

[1]   DeCusatis, C., Carranza, A., & Delgado-Caceres, J. (2016). Modeling Software Defined Networks using Mininet. Proc. 2nd Int. Conf. Comput. Inf. Sci. Technol. Ottawa, Canada,

[2]   Emmons, m. a. (2021). Scapy – Packet Manipulation in Kali Linux. geeksforgeeks.org. Retrieved 15 Apr,2022 from https://www.geeksforgeeks.or g/scapy-packet-manipulation-in-kali-linux/

[3]   Kodzai, C. (2020). Impact of network security on SDN controller performance University of Cape Town.

[4]   Patel, P. (July 5, 2016). Implementing software-defined network (SDN) based firewall. Nirma University. Retrieved April 19, 2022 from https://www. opensourceforu.com/2016/07/implementing-a-softwaredefined-network-sdn-based-firewall/

4

Implementation and Testing

This chapter bridges the gap between theoretical design and practical application, guiding you through the crucial process of setting up a test environment to assess the effectiveness of the proposed entropy-based detection system for SDN security.

First, we embark on a step-by-step journey, equipping you with the knowledge and tools to create a comprehensive test environment. From selecting appropriate hardware and software to configuring the network infrastructure, this guide ensures you have a robust platform for simulating real-world scenarios. By following these clear instructions, you gain the practical skills needed to replicate your own SDN environment within a controlled setting.

Next, we explore the world of simulated DDoS attacks. Where you can learn how to craft realistic attack scenarios within your test environment, mimicking the tactics and behaviors of real-world adversaries. By simulating diverse attack vectors, you gain valuable insights into the system's ability to detect and respond to a wide range of threats, ensuring its robustness and adaptability. Finally, we evaluate the effectiveness of the proposed methodology. By analyzing the outcomes of the testing phase, we delve into the system's performance metrics, accuracy rates, and overall effectiveness in identifying and mitigating DDoS attacks. Witnessing these results provides concrete evidence of the system's capabilities, empowering you to make informed decisions about its suitability for your own security needs.

This chapter serves as a practical guide for security professionals, network administrators, and researchers alike. In this chapter, we will go through the tools used in the design process, as well as the integration points for submodules and the deployment of the solution in a virtual environment. The chapter provides an overview of the technologies employed in the control plane infrastructure with the POX controller.

4.1 Setting Up a Test Environment

In this section, we will discuss the testbed and overall design, which includes the hardware and physical architecture, logical network design, and control to data plane designs.

This section outlines the suggested entropy-based method for mitigating DDoS traffic and the hosts' related targets with the design components with the high-level design and requirements of the discrete components that comprise the prototype creating the security solution under evaluation in this book in the previous chapter. As previously stated, the suggested security solution is based on the SDN controller, which is the primary target of attacks in SDN technology. The suggested technology is implemented in a simulated environment to validate it.

In principle, an OpenFlow controller is linked to a network, and the entropy of traffic associated with the controller is measured under normal and attack conditions. The system module of Python was used in the research to access system-specific parameters and functions.

This section examines how these tools are used to deliver the following key design areas: physical layout design, network logical design, design implementation for DDoS detection and mitigation, and design implementation for interoperability of SDN environment applications as depicted in Figure 4.1.

For the Windows environment, the most recent version of Virtual Box was downloaded. After installing a suitable version of Virtual Box, a Mininet VM image was downloaded. Mininet can be used to build realistic virtual networks. Mininet allows you to experiment with OpenFlow and software defined networks. Mininet has been used to implement a virtual network topology in order to simulate a real-world environment. Mininet allows for the creation of custom topologies. Because of the power of virtualization, a single system can be made to appear to be a network. The SSH tool is used to access the virtual machine's command line from the physical machine via port 22; its use is not required, but it facilitates the copying of codes and scripts between the two machines.

Figure 4.1: Design setup for physical and testbed layout.

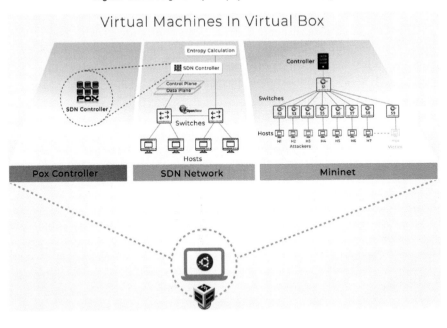

It includes the physical layout of Ubuntu in VirtualBox, POX controller, SDN Network, and Mininet in the virtualization environment for easy traffic flow interpretation and logic. The specific system requirements and the highest system resources in terms of RAM and CPU used in physical and virtual machines were demonstrated in Appendix A4.

4.1.1 Network topology modeling

The network topology described in Chapter 3, which is a treelike structure, is implemented and used as a reference for the definition of the test scenario This topology was chosen because it is a network structure that is commonly used in data centers and has been used in research related to this work.

It is necessary to set up a network for the test, and the command used to do so is listed below, from within the Mininet environment. By running and entering the following command which is used to generate and create the proposed topology:

$ sudo mn –switch ovsk –topo tree, depth=2, fanout=8 –controller= remote, ip=192.168.137.16, port=6633.

This command establishes a network and configures it with controllers, hosts, switches, and links shown in Figure 4.2, where a tree-type topology is generated with the following network elements: One controller (c0), nine OVS switches (s1, s2, s3...) and sixty-four hosts (h1, h2, h3...).

Figure 4.2: Designing the network topology.

```
wendina@VirtualBox:~$ sudo mn --switch ovsk --topo tree,depth=2,fanout=8 --controller=remote,ip=192.168.137.16
,port=6633
*** Creating network
*** Adding controller
*** Adding hosts:
h1 h2 h3 h4 h5 h6 h7 h8 h9 h10 h11 h12 h13 h14 h15 h16 h17 h18 h19 h20 h21 h22 h23 h24 h25 h26 h27 h28 h29 h30
 h31 h32 h33 h34 h35 h36 h37 h38 h39 h40 h41 h42 h43 h44 h45 h46 h47 h48 h49 h50 h51 h52 h53 h54 h55 h56 h57 h
58 h59 h60 h61 h62 h63 h64
*** Adding switches:
s1 s2 s3 s4 s5 s6 s7 s8 s9
*** Adding links:
(s1, s2) (s1, s3) (s1, s4) (s1, s5) (s1, s6) (s1, s7) (s1, s8) (s1, s9) (s2, h1) (s2, h2) (s2, h3) (s2, h4) (s
2, h5) (s2, h6) (s2, h7) (s2, h8) (s3, h9) (s3, h10) (s3, h11) (s3, h12) (s3, h13) (s3, h14) (s3, h15) (s3, h1
6) (s4, h17) (s4, h18) (s4, h19) (s4, h20) (s4, h21) (s4, h22) (s4, h23) (s4, h24) (s5, h25) (s5, h26) (s5, h2
7) (s5, h28) (s5, h29) (s5, h30) (s5, h31) (s5, h32) (s6, h33) (s6, h34) (s6, h35) (s6, h36) (s6, h37) (s6, h3
8) (s6, h39) (s6, h40) (s7, h41) (s7, h42) (s7, h43) (s7, h44) (s7, h45) (s7, h46) (s7, h47) (s7, h48) (s8, h4
9) (s8, h50) (s8, h51) (s8, h52) (s8, h53) (s8, h54) (s8, h55) (s8, h56) (s9, h57) (s9, h58) (s9, h59) (s9, h6
0) (s9, h61) (s9, h62) (s9, h63) (s9, h64)
*** Configuring hosts
h1 h2 h3 h4 h5 h6 h7 h8 h9 h10 h11 h12 h13 h14 h15 h16 h17 h18 h19 h20 h21 h22 h23 h24 h25 h26 h27 h28 h29 h30
 h31 h32 h33 h34 h35 h36 h37 h38 h39 h40 h41 h42 h43 h44 h45 h46 h47 h48 h49 h50 h51 h52 h53 h54 h55 h56 h57 h
58 h59 h60 h61 h62 h63 h64
*** Starting controller
c0
*** Starting 9 switches
s1 s2 s3 s4 s5 s6 s7 s8 s9 ...
*** Starting CLI:
mininet>
```

The respective network links are automatically generated. Mininet can also be used to generate the topology by selecting each of the elements with their respective network links, attackers, and victim hosts. Figure 4.2 depicts the network topology in Mininet; in this case, a single host has been represented per level 2 switch to facilitate visualization by considering the following table of Mininet launch parameters.

The preceding command will generate a topology with 64 hosts linked to 9 switches. Each of the nine switches is built on port 6633 and has an IP address that matches the provided IP address or loopback IP address in the previous statement. Each packet may be examined by the switch, and the source port mapping can be learned. Following that, the port will be assigned the source MAC address. If the packet's destination is already connected with a port, the packet will be forwarded to that port; otherwise, it will be flooded on all ports of the switch. The data path id identifies each open flow switch. The switch can discard packets on a flow, either immediately or completely, based on the controller's commands. Packet dropping can be used to protect against DDoS

Table 4.1: Mininet startup settings.

Parameter Reference	Configuration	Comment
Topology	−topo tree, depth =2	Tree topology
Controller	Controller = remote, ip = 192.168.137.16	Remote controller in VM with IP address 192.168 .137 .16
Southbound Protocol	Openflow13	Connect using OpenFlow version 1.3
Port	Port = 6633	Include port address of controller

attacks. POX establishes a methodology for interacting with SDN switches. The OpenFlow protocol was employed in this case. POX must be launched from the command line, and a layer 3 switch has been installed.

As described, the POX controller was chosen from among the available controllers for this work. The pox driver is installed automatically with the Mininet tool in this project, the same virtual machine as the OpenFlow driver is used, though it is also possible to run it from a different virtual machine. Figure 4.3 illustrates the network components in MiniEdit that are used to represent network nodes.

Figure 4.3: MiniEdit nodes.

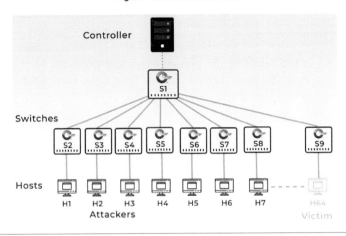

The default driver is configured with the IP address 10.1.1.1 and port 6634, so it is necessary to configure it with the IP address of the machine that you want to act as the controller. This is configured by using the command:

wendina@virtualbox: ∼$. /pox.py openflow. of_01 - - address=192.168.137.16 - - port=6633

Then it is necessary to activate by the command line to the POX controller with the help of the command:

wendina@virtualbox: ∼$ python3./pox/pox.py forwarding. l3_editing

Figure 4.4 demonstrates the successful activation of the controller with its respective version, as well as a summary of the switches connected to it. There can be no network convergence if this step is skipped.

Figure 4.4: Activating the POX controller.

```
wendina@virtualbox:~$ python3 ./pox/pox.py forwarding.l3_editing
POX 0.7.0 (gar) / Copyright 2011-2020 James McCauley, et al.
WARNING:version:Support for Python 3 is experimental.
INFO:core:POX 0.7.0 (gar) is up.
INFO:openflow.of_01:[00-00-00-00-00-06 1] connected
INFO:openflow.of_01:[00-00-00-00-00-01 2] connected
INFO:openflow.of_01:[00-00-00-00-00-03 3] connected
INFO:openflow.of_01:[00-00-00-00-00-08 4] connected
INFO:openflow.of_01:[00-00-00-00-00-02 5] connected
INFO:openflow.of_01:[00-00-00-00-00-09 6] connected
INFO:openflow.of_01:[00-00-00-00-00-07 7] connected
INFO:openflow.of_01:[00-00-00-00-00-04 8] connected
INFO:openflow.of_01:[00-00-00-00-00-05 9] connected
```

Figure 4.5 is the result of the pingall command executed on the Mininet command line, it is observed that all packets have been successfully received denoting the convergence of the network.

This command is a simple way to check connectivity between hosts on the network, although it is also possible to use the ping command from each terminal. Start the POX controller and design a Mininet topology to check cross host connectivity.

Figure 4.5: Cross-host connectivity check.

```
                    wendina@VirtualBox: ~/mininet/custom        Q  =   _  □  ✕

  wendina@VirtualBox: ~/mininet/custom  ×    wendina@VirtualBox: ~/mininet/examp...  ×   ▼

h58 -> h1 h2 h3 h4 h5 h6 h7 h8 h9 h10 h11 h12 h13 h14 h15 h16 h17 h18 h19 h20 h21 h2
2 h23 h24 h25 h26 h27 h28 h29 h30 h31 h32 h33 h34 h35 h36 h37 h38 h39 h40 h41 h42 h4
3 h44 h45 h46 h47 h48 h49 h50 h51 h52 h53 h54 h55 h56 h57 h59 h60 h61 h62 h63 h64
h59 -> h1 h2 h3 h4 h5 h6 h7 h8 h9 h10 h11 h12 h13 h14 h15 h16 h17 h18 h19 h20 h21 h2
2 h23 h24 h25 h26 h27 h28 h29 h30 h31 h32 h33 h34 h35 h36 h37 h38 h39 h40 h41 h42 h4
3 h44 h45 h46 h47 h48 h49 h50 h51 h52 h53 h54 h55 h56 h57 h58 h60 h61 h62 h63 h64
h60 -> h1 h2 h3 h4 h5 h6 h7 h8 h9 h10 h11 h12 h13 h14 h15 h16 h17 h18 h19 h20 h21 h2
2 h23 h24 h25 h26 h27 h28 h29 h30 h31 h32 h33 h34 h35 h36 h37 h38 h39 h40 h41 h42 h4
3 h44 h45 h46 h47 h48 h49 h50 h51 h52 h53 h54 h55 h56 h57 h58 h59 h61 h62 h63 h64
h61 -> h1 h2 h3 h4 h5 h6 h7 h8 h9 h10 h11 h12 h13 h14 h15 h16 h17 h18 h19 h20 h21 h2
2 h23 h24 h25 h26 h27 h28 h29 h30 h31 h32 h33 h34 h35 h36 h37 h38 h39 h40 h41 h42 h4
3 h44 h45 h46 h47 h48 h49 h50 h51 h52 h53 h54 h55 h56 h57 h58 h59 h60 h62 h63 h64
h62 -> h1 h2 h3 h4 h5 h6 h7 h8 h9 h10 h11 h12 h13 h14 h15 h16 h17 h18 h19 h20 h21 h2
2 h23 h24 h25 h26 h27 h28 h29 h30 h31 h32 h33 h34 h35 h36 h37 h38 h39 h40 h41 h42 h4
3 h44 h45 h46 h47 h48 h49 h50 h51 h52 h53 h54 h55 h56 h57 h58 h59 h60 h61 h63 h64
h63 -> h1 h2 h3 h4 h5 h6 h7 h8 h9 h10 h11 h12 h13 h14 h15 h16 h17 h18 h19 h20 h21 h2
2 h23 h24 h25 h26 h27 h28 h29 h30 h31 h32 h33 h34 h35 h36 h37 h38 h39 h40 h41 h42 h4
3 h44 h45 h46 h47 h48 h49 h50 h51 h52 h53 h54 h55 h56 h57 h58 h59 h60 h61 h62 h64
h64 -> h1 h2 h3 h4 h5 h6 h7 h8 h9 h10 h11 h12 h13 h14 h15 h16 h17 h18 h19 h20 h21 h2
2 h23 h24 h25 h26 h27 h28 h29 h30 h31 h32 h33 h34 h35 h36 h37 h38 h39 h40 h41 h42 h4
3 h44 h45 h46 h47 h48 h49 h50 h51 h52 h53 h54 h55 h56 h57 h58 h59 h60 h61 h62 h63
*** Results: 0% dropped (4032/4032 received)
mininet>
```

4.2 Simulating DDoS Attacks

The preceding chapter describes the different tools, protocols, and technologies
necessary to build the proof-of-concept model for the proposed entropy-based
network security solution for the POX controller. This section will assess the
security solution's efficacy and efficiency against DDoS assaults, as well as
the security solution's influence on controller performance. The efficacy of the
security solution is determined by determining whether or not the mitigation
of DDoS packets from a DDoS producing server was successful. The user must
specify the range of IP addresses for the destination IP address. For example,
if the user sends the number from 1 to 256. The IP addresses will then be
produced in the format 10.0.0.D, where D will be between the start and end
values supplied. A function will generate the source IP address at random.
The packets will be delivered across the network using the Scapy Python
module after the source and destination IP addresses have been set. The SDN
network was set up in each test, the communication between elements was

validated, and the POX performance results were recorded and captured for analysis.

Scapy is the program used to produce both legitimate and malicious traffic. This application may be launched from a terminal window as well as by executing scripts. For this project, two scripts have been written: one for normal or legitimate traffic flows and one for attack flows. UDP is the packet type used for both normal and attack communication. Mininet successively allocates IP addresses to hosts beginning with 10.0.0.1. The destination IP address is created based on the range given in the script (10. 0.0.1–10.0.0.64) for normal traffic, while the source IP address is generated randomly using the randrange random function. Figures 4.6 and 4.7 show the generation of normal traffic by implementing a script from a host.

Figure 4.6: Legitimate traffic generation for h1.

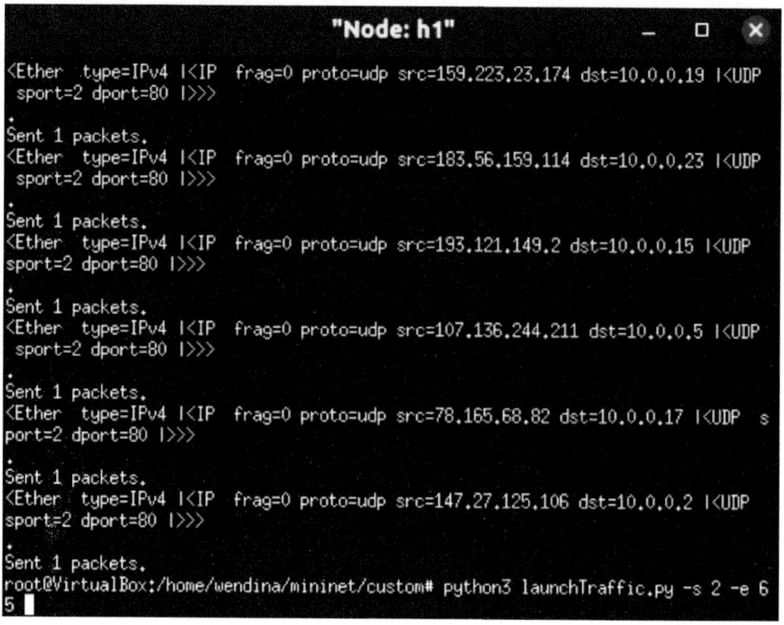

```
                          "Node: h1"              —   □   ✕

<Ether  type=IPv4 |<IP  frag=0 proto=udp src=159.223.23.174 dst=10.0.0.19 |<UDP
   sport=2 dport=80 |>>>
.
Sent 1 packets.
<Ether  type=IPv4 |<IP  frag=0 proto=udp src=183.56.159.114 dst=10.0.0.23 |<UDP
   sport=2 dport=80 |>>>
.
Sent 1 packets.
<Ether  type=IPv4 |<IP  frag=0 proto=udp src=193.121.149.2 dst=10.0.0.15 |<UDP
  sport=2 dport=80 |>>>
.
Sent 1 packets.
<Ether  type=IPv4 |<IP  frag=0 proto=udp src=107.136.244.211 dst=10.0.0.5 |<UDP
   sport=2 dport=80 |>>>
.
Sent 1 packets.
<Ether  type=IPv4 |<IP  frag=0 proto=udp src=78.165.68.82 dst=10.0.0.17 |<UDP  s
  port=2 dport=80 |>>>
.
Sent 1 packets.
<Ether  type=IPv4 |<IP  frag=0 proto=udp src=147.27.125.106 dst=10.0.0.2 |<UDP
  sport=2 dport=80 |>>>
.
Sent 1 packets.
root@VirtualBox:/home/wendina/mininet/custom# python3 launchTraffic.py -s 2 -e 6
5 ▊
```

Figure 4.7: Legitimate traffic generation for h64.

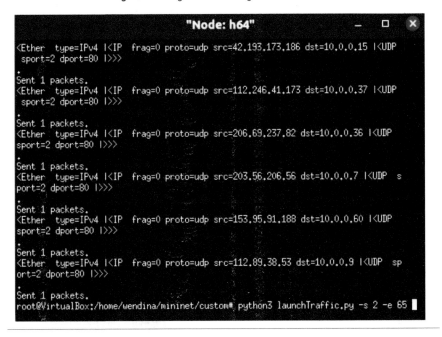

4.2.1 Launch Traffic and Verification

The inputs "2" and "65" are passed to the generate destination IP function, which produces the destination IP addresses. The launch traffic function, in principle produces random source addresses and sends packets to random destinations between the hosts. Generally, supply the start and end values from one of the node's command prompts, for example h1, h64.

Wireshark was chosen as a tool for visualizing the packets. Using Wireshark, the loopback interface was monitored prior to any communication on the loopback to achieve this status. Figure 4.8 displays the capturing of legitimate traffic from another network and the data was captured using I/O graphs in Wireshark.

Figure 4.8: Legitimate traffic scenario.

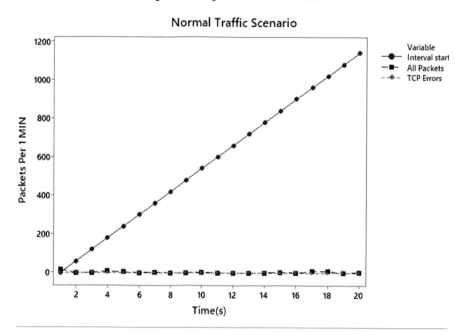

Normal Traffic Scenario

4.2.2 Launch attack and verification

In this case, initiate the attack from a few selected hosts to a single target. The controller's entropy value is now decreasing. In this section, it provides the target IP address from the command prompt of the hosts that are working as a botnet. To carry out the attack on a specific host, the packet generation script must be run using random source IP addresses. Consider the entropy numbers in the pox controller. The number is lower than the previously specified normal traffic thresholds. As a result, the attack may be detected within the first 250 packets of malicious data targeted at a given host in the SDN network. When performing the command, the victim's IP address is supplied, as illustrated in Figures 4.9, 4.10 and 4.11. Repeating the steps in Section 4.2.1 on hosts h1 and h64 while simultaneously providing the following syntax to execute the attack traffic from h1, h2,h3 in xterm windows respectively to attack on 10.0.0.2 and 10.0.0.64 that attack packets are going to be sent to this destination IP address. The primary purpose of this module is to demonstrate how a malicious user might attempt to attack a network resource.

Figure 4.9: Attack traffic generation on h1 to 10.0.0.64.

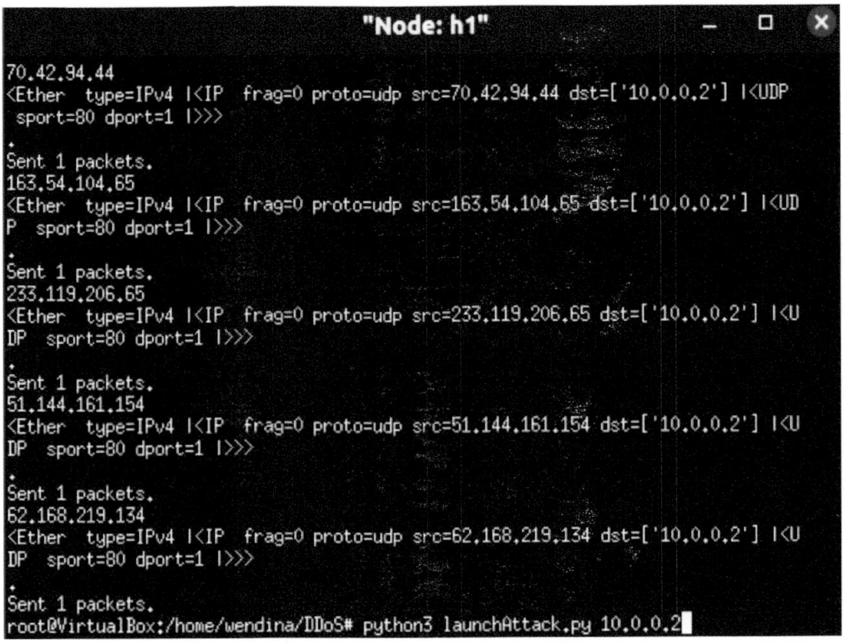

Figure 4.10: Attack traffic generation on h2 to 10.0.0.64.

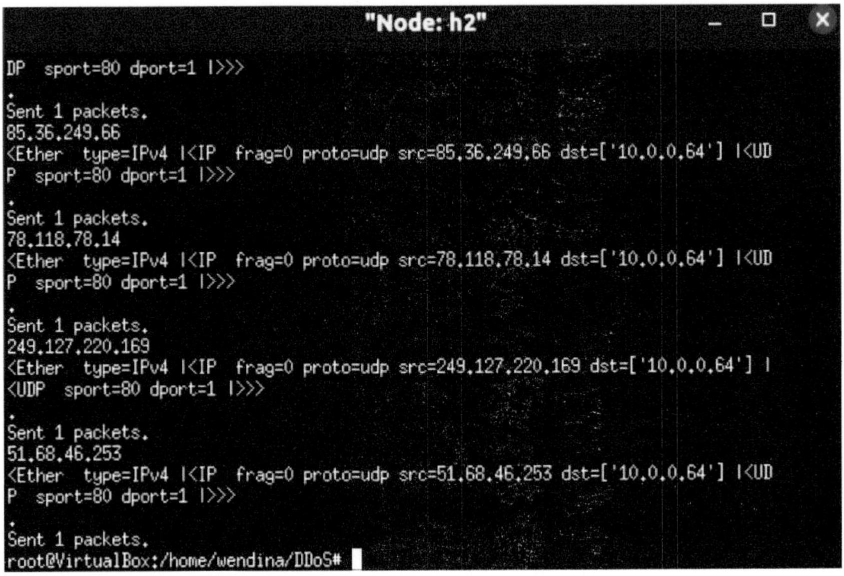

Figure 4.11: Attack traffic generation on h3 to 10.0.0.64.

```
                        "Node: h3"              —    ▢    ⊗

<Ether  type=IPv4  I<IP  frag=0 proto=udp src=40.8.135.94 dst=['10.0.0.64']  I<UDP
    sport=80 dport=1 I>>>
.
Sent 1 packets.
221.214.94.116
<Ether  type=IPv4  I<IP  frag=0 proto=udp src=221.214.94.116 dst=['10.0.0.64']  I<
UDP  sport=80 dport=1 I>>>
.
Sent 1 packets.
81.244.138.43
<Ether  type=IPv4  I<IP  frag=0 proto=udp src=81.244.138.43 dst=['10.0.0.64']  I<U
IP   sport=80 dport=1 I>>>
.
Sent 1 packets.
197.148.220.243
<Ether  type=IPv4  I<IP  frag=0 proto=udp src=197.148.220.243 dst=['10.0.0.64']  I
<UDP   sport=80 dport=1 I>>>
.
Sent 1 packets.
240.185.15.190
<Ether  type=IPv4  I<IP  frag=0 proto=udp src=240.185.15.190 dst=['10.0.0.64']  I<
UDP  sport=80 dport=1 I>>>
.
Sent 1 packets.
root@VirtualBox:/home/wendina/DDoS# python3 launchAttack.py 10.0.0.64
```

The capturing of attack traffic from another host and the data generated was interpreted using I/O graphs in Wireshark in similar manner to legitimate traffic which was discussed previously. The graph in Figure 4.12 depicts network traffic over time. Only one host was utilized to produce attack traffic over here. The amplitude on the y-axis would have been greater if more than one host had been used and the attack TCP packets directed towards the host with address 10.0.0.64. The source addresses are random and correspond to the ranges set in the script.

The simulation of the network along with the DDoS attacks was detailed in Sections 4.1 and 4.2. The chosen solution requires only the controller because the detection and mitigation of DDoS attacks is done by programming it. The detection of DDoS threats using the wntropy value before and after the DDoS attack may be evaluated. The detection module is responsible for calculating the entropy of the network, which is greater than one because there is only normal traffic (see Figure 4.13) and takes values less than 0.5 when there is an attack in progress (see Figure 4.14).

Analyzing the POX controller's entropy levels. The number falls below the threshold for normal traffic (0.5 in this case). As a consequence, it may identify

Figure 4.12: Attack traffic scenario.

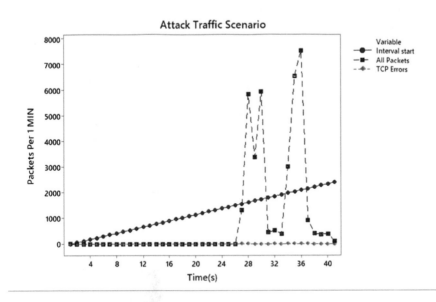

Figure 4.13: Entropy with normal traffic.

```
INFO:forwarding.detection:Entropy =
INFO:forwarding.detection:1.19650210303
INFO:forwarding.detection:Entropy =
INFO:forwarding.detection:1.23048150312
INFO:forwarding.detection:Entropy =
INFO:forwarding.detection:1.2644609032
INFO:forwarding.detection:Entropy =
INFO:forwarding.detection:1.29844030329
INFO:forwarding.detection:Entropy =
INFO:forwarding.detection:1.33241970338
INFO:forwarding.detection:Entropy =
INFO:forwarding.detection:1.36639910346
INFO:forwarding.detection:Entropy =
INFO:forwarding.detection:1.43971002844
INFO:forwarding.detection:Entropy =
INFO:forwarding.detection:1.47368942853
INFO:forwarding.detection:Entropy =
INFO:forwarding.detection:1.50766882861
INFO:forwarding.detection:{IPAddr('10.0.0.36'): 1, IPAddr('10.0.0.44'): 1, IPAddr('10.0.0.52'): 1
, IPAddr('10.0.0.64'): 1, IPAddr('10.0.0.5'): 1, IPAddr('10.0.0.6'): 2, IPAddr('10.0.0.14'): 1, I
PAddr('10.0.0.25'): 1, IPAddr('10.0.0.3'): 1, IPAddr('10.0.0.50'): 1, IPAddr('10.0.0.62'): 1, IPA
ddr('10.0.0.8'): 3, IPAddr('10.0.0.11'): 2, IPAddr('10.0.0.51'): 3, IPAddr('10.0.0.59'): 3, IPAdd
r('10.0.0.43'): 1, IPAddr('10.0.0.32'): 1, IPAddr('10.0.0.40'): 1, IPAddr('10.0.0.48'): 1, IPAddr
('10.0.0.60'): 1, IPAddr('10.0.0.54'): 1, IPAddr('10.0.0.2'): 2, IPAddr('10.0.0.10'): 1, IPAddr('
10.0.0.18'): 2, IPAddr('10.0.0.21'): 3, IPAddr('10.0.0.61'): 1, IPAddr('10.0.0.55'): 1, IPAddr('1
0.0.0.34'): 1, IPAddr('10.0.0.15'): 1, IPAddr('10.0.0.46'): 1, IPAddr('10.0.0.30'): 1, IPAddr('10
.0.0.58'): 1, IPAddr('10.0.0.20'): 1, IPAddr('10.0.0.7'): 3, IPAddr('10.0.0.41'): 1, IPAddr('10.0
.0.22'): 1}

***** Entropy Value =  1.50766882861 *****
```

Figure 4.14: Entropy with an ongoing DDoS attack.

```
***** Entropy Value =  0.555604456968 *****


***** Entropy Value =  0.555604456968 *****

INFO:forwarding.detection:Entropy =
INFO:forwarding.detection:0.0339794000867
INFO:forwarding.detection:Entropy =
INFO:forwarding.detection:0.153086402629
INFO:forwarding.detection:Entropy =
INFO:forwarding.detection:0.187059802716
INFO:forwarding.detection:Entropy =
INFO:forwarding.detection:0.3439234263
INFO:forwarding.detection:{IPAddr('10.0.0.36'): 1, IPAddr('10.0.0.64'): 33, IPAddr('10.0.0.48'): 1,
IPAddr('10.0.0.2'): 15}

***** Entropy Value =  0.3439234263 *****
```

an attack within the first 250 packets of malicious traffic detected by a host in the SDN network.

4.3 Evaluating the Effectiveness of the Methodology

This section analyzes one of the outcomes of the following sequential phases such as risk identification, planning, mechanism selection, testing, implementation monitoring, and improvement. The main goal is to carry out the installation of the chosen solution into the organization's infrastructure. Thus, technical compliance with the detection and mitigation of DDoS attacks in SDN environments based on the entropy standard is believed to enhance control plane security. This is the approach of this work, because it was specified in the scope that only a controlled simulation scenario would be employed. In a real case, the implementation would be done in the SDN controller by developing a detection module and altering the POX controller's l3 learning.py file in the same way that it was done in the test scenario. It was created based on what was done in the simulation scenario, explaining the configurations done on the SDN controller that might be used in a real controller.

Figure 4.15 shows the detection and mitigation of the attack on the SDN controller, this scenario corresponds to an attack on host 64 from hosts 2 and 3, while host1 generates legitimate traffic. When the entropy value decreases from the set limit (0.5), the controller displays a message indicating that an attack is in progress and proceeds to block the switch port from which the attack comes, in this case port 1 of the switch 2.

Figure 4.15: DDoS attack detection and mitigation.

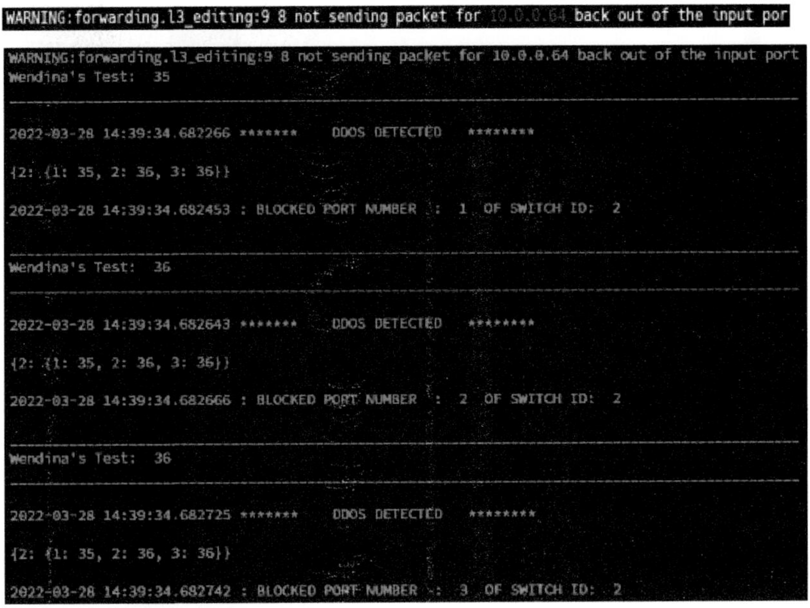

```
WARNING:forwarding.l3_editing:9 8 not sending packet for 10.0.0.64 back out of the input por
```

```
WARNING:forwarding.l3_editing:9 8 not sending packet for 10.0.0.64 back out of the input port
Wendina's Test:   35

2022-03-28 14:39:34.682266 ******   DDOS DETECTED   ********

{2: {1: 35, 2: 36, 3: 36}}

2022-03-28 14:39:34.682453 : BLOCKED PORT NUMBER  :  1  OF SWITCH ID:  2

Wendina's Test:   36

2022-03-28 14:39:34.682643 ****** DDOS DETECTED   ********

{2: {1: 35, 2: 36, 3: 36}}

2022-03-28 14:39:34.682666 : BLOCKED PORT NUMBER  :  2  OF SWITCH ID:  2

Wendina's Test:   36

2022-03-28 14:39:34.682725 ****** DDOS DETECTED   ********

{2: {1: 35, 2: 36, 3: 36}}

2022-03-28 14:39:34.682742 : BLOCKED PORT NUMBER  :  3  OF SWITCH ID:  2
```

It can be seen that port number 2 of switch 2 has been blocked to prevent further harm from being caused by the attack. Looking through the dictionary, you'll note that port 1 of switch 2 has been activated 35 times. Switch 2's similar port 3 has been activated 36 times. These are direct signs of an attack, and the application will block these ports if it detects that the network is under attack.

Analysis of DDoS mitigation impact on the POX controller and attack traffic with prevention using proposed algorithm that detects the attack network and can be compared with its equivalents resulted as shown in Figures 4.16 and 4.17 of an entropy algorithm and an association algorithm respectively.

Figure 4.18 shows the measurement of entropy in the scenario posed during the test. Initially without current traffic in the network the entropy had the value of 1, when generating legitimate traffic, the entropy amounted to 1.5. At the time of generating the DDoS attack towards host 64 the value of the entropy dropped to 0.4. The graph shows that from the time the attack is generated (4.5 s) until it is detected (6.5 s) approximately two seconds pass, this being an early detection. it is clear that the attack traffic with the mitigation approach applied in this research can achieve a greater entropy decrease rate and has the function of quick detection.

Figure 4.16: Attack traffic with mitigation, entropy algorithm.

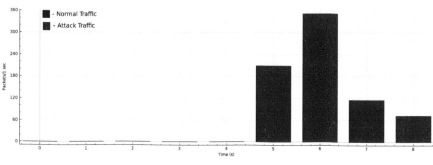

Figure 4.17: Attack traffic with mitigation, association algorithm.

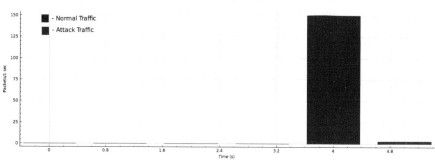

Figure 4.18: Entropy variations and measurement.

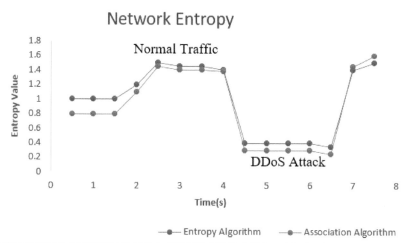

When one host receives many more packets than the other, the entropy value decreases. As a result, the entropy falls below the prior limit of one. The decrease in entropy value shows inconsistency in network traffic. This dictionary is generated only when the entropy value is less than 0.5. The essential values in our Mininet topology correlate to the switches. The keys in the value dictionaries correspond to the needed switch's ports. The final value is the number of times the ports have been activated. This is another reliable sign of unexpected network behavior that could indicate the existence of a DDoS attack. It was designed to track detection time since it is the factor that influences whether detection and mitigation are carried out early in the attack.

If this were a real-world situation, the monitoring would be carried out within the time frame given in the planning, observing the performance of the developed solution against real-world attacks on the controller. Because this was a controller test scenario, the monitoring was done by producing various forms of TCP, UDP, and ICMP attack traffic.

Reviewing the logs generated in the controller interface produced the detection time. The network administrator was described as the person in charge of doing the monitoring and interpreting the data. Monitoring results against different TCP, UDP, and ICMP flood DDoS attacks were recorded. TCP protocol synchronization request packets (SYN) with random source IP addresses and a specified destination (victim) IP address were generated for the TCP Flood attack, also known as SYN Flood. A Wireshark capture of the packets generated for this attack is shown in Figure 4.19.

Figure 4.19: TCP flood attack.

No.	Time	Source	Destination	Protocol	Length	Info
798	38.148825063	72.167.139.21	10.0.0.64	TCP	54	2 → 80 [SYN] Seq
799	38.180567964	13.117.90.128	10.0.0.64	TCP	54	2 → 80 [SYN] Seq
800	38.215500797	114.85.113.143	10.0.0.64	TCP	54	2 → 80 [SYN] Seq
801	38.251180729	109.138.220.113	10.0.0.64	TCP	54	2 → 80 [SYN] Seq
802	38.283002108	99.233.85.32	10.0.0.64	TCP	54	2 → 80 [SYN] Seq
803	38.312817793	247.102.172.141	10.0.0.64	TCP	54	2 → 80 [SYN] Seq
804	38.343965763	67.135.204.24	10.0.0.64	TCP	54	2 → 80 [SYN] Seq
805	38.372318285	150.213.114.199	10.0.0.64	TCP	54	2 → 80 [SYN] Seq
806	38.401875790	34.224.66.135	10.0.0.64	TCP	54	2 → 80 [SYN] Seq
807	38.432022720	84.21.62.188	10.0.0.64	TCP	54	2 → 80 [SYN] Seq
808	38.460469362	182.6.177.166	10.0.0.64	TCP	54	2 → 80 [SYN] Seq
809	38.494801176	160.164.105.193	10.0.0.64	TCP	54	2 → 80 [SYN] Seq
810	38.527416739	178.131.191.3	10.0.0.64	TCP	54	2 → 80 [SYN] Seq
811	38.574467185	162.169.155.18	10.0.0.64	TCP	54	2 → 80 [SYN] Seq
812	38.605612586	51.235.149.81	10.0.0.64	TCP	54	2 → 80 [SYN] Seq
813	38.636257175	80.231.131.157	10.0.0.64	TCP	54	2 → 80 [SYN] Seq
814	38.667898869	176.216.187.193	10.0.0.64	TCP	54	2 → 80 [SYN] Seq
815	38.696431697	217.13.101.180	10.0.0.64	TCP	54	2 → 80 [SYN] Seq
816	38.726104888	119.229.236.39	10.0.0.64	TCP	54	2 → 80 [SYN] Seq

The UDP flood attack was created in the same way as the TCP flood attack, except that the UDP protocol was utilized and tested with different ports of destination that correspond to typical services that handle this protocol, such as port 53/UDP (DNS). Figure 4.20 demonstrates a Wireshark capture of the packets transmitted in this attack.

Figure 4.20: UDP flood attack.

No.	Time	Source	Destination	Protocol	Length	Info
2293	162.941497807	183.180.130.218	10.0.0.64	UDP	42	53 → 53 L
2294	162.971582798	82.207.134.79	10.0.0.64	UDP	42	53 → 53 L
2295	163.002777052	141.92.82.36	10.0.0.64	UDP	42	53 → 53 L
2296	163.033778409	84.3.42.86	10.0.0.64	UDP	42	53 → 53 L
2297	163.064299358	153.243.108.129	10.0.0.64	UDP	42	53 → 53 L
2298	163.098929539	180.194.11.36	10.0.0.64	UDP	42	53 → 53 L
2299	163.128455258	92.67.159.113	10.0.0.64	UDP	42	53 → 53 L
2300	163.159855541	233.14.254.64	10.0.0.64	UDP	42	53 → 53 L
2301	163.191294437	129.17.84.221	10.0.0.64	UDP	42	53 → 53 L
2302	163.222926918	128.151.220.153	10.0.0.64	UDP	42	53 → 53 L
2303	163.251258935	120.112.150.175	10.0.0.64	UDP	42	53 → 53 L
2304	163.282579771	6.144.168.173	10.0.0.64	UDP	42	53 → 53 L
2305	163.314115539	101.144.61.132	10.0.0.64	UDP	42	53 → 53 L
2306	163.344757167	20.212.10.121	10.0.0.64	UDP	42	53 → 53 L
2307	163.383168217	130.213.63.61	10.0.0.64	UDP	42	53 → 53 L
2308	163.411537072	20.155.46.190	10.0.0.64	UDP	42	53 → 53 L
2309	163.442778110	250.75.174.246	10.0.0.64	UDP	42	53 → 53 L
2310	163.471178632	221.227.95.54	10.0.0.64	UDP	42	53 → 53 L
2311	163.500677685	163.95.194.252	10.0.0.64	UDP	42	53 → 53 L

For the ICMP flood attack, Echo request packets were generated, which use the ICMP protocol. Wireshark's capture of the packets generated in this attack is shown in Figure 4.21.

Figure 4.21: ICMP flood attack.

No.	Time	Source	Destination	Protocol	Length	Info
3158	213.347800863	131.184.98.155	10.0.0.64	ICMP	42	Echo (ping) request id=(
3159	213.376523621	156.25.62.214	10.0.0.64	ICMP	42	Echo (ping) request id=(
3160	213.427846024	245.139.1.70	10.0.0.64	ICMP	42	Echo (ping) request id=(
3161	213.456659048	191.87.115.160	10.0.0.64	ICMP	42	Echo (ping) request id=(
3162	213.495504959	31.19.227.255	10.0.0.64	ICMP	42	Echo (ping) request id=(
3163	213.527504432	123.107.242.238	10.0.0.64	ICMP	42	Echo (ping) request id=(
3164	213.557278202	27.70.199.91	10.0.0.64	ICMP	42	Echo (ping) request id=(
3165	213.589692285	167.203.56.243	10.0.0.64	ICMP	42	Echo (ping) request id=(
3166	213.622753353	126.28.81.23	10.0.0.64	ICMP	42	Echo (ping) request id=(
3167	213.652716765	15.65.117.44	10.0.0.64	ICMP	42	Echo (ping) request id=(
3168	213.683801724	128.12.232.86	10.0.0.64	ICMP	42	Echo (ping) request id=(
3169	213.723062401	218.247.143.181	10.0.0.64	ICMP	42	Echo (ping) request id=(
3170	213.757689331	52.25.73.62	10.0.0.64	ICMP	42	Echo (ping) request id=(
3171	213.790915129	40.70.81.28	10.0.0.64	ICMP	42	Echo (ping) request id=(
3172	213.868447264	81.189.176.231	10.0.0.64	ICMP	42	Echo (ping) request id=(
3173	213.905246615	201.193.212.83	10.0.0.64	ICMP	42	Echo (ping) request id=(
3174	213.936934550	155.210.236.67	10.0.0.64	ICMP	42	Echo (ping) request id=(
3175	213.973817691	87.37.64.194	10.0.0.64	ICMP	42	Echo (ping) request id=(
3176	214.004911812	235.66.119.90	10.0.0.64	ICMP	42	Echo (ping) request id=(

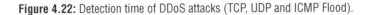
Figure 4.22: Detection time of DDoS attacks (TCP, UDP and ICMP Flood).

Figure 4.22 indicates that the detection of DDoS attacks using the implemented mechanism is independent of the packet type, since the same is obtained detection time (2 s) for all three types of simulated attacks. This is because the mechanism used is based on the destination IP address to measure the entropy of the network. SYN flood is one of the most common DDoS attacks observed and it occurs when an attacker sends a succession of transmission control protocol (TCP) synchronization requests (SYN) to the target. A UDP flood attack is similar to a SYN flood in that a botnet is used to send a large amount of traffic to the destination server.

It was concluded that the solution meets the objectives set out in the planning; however, a disagreement was found regarding the excessive number of messages in the controller terminal that prevents the network administrator from monitoring the events reported by the controller. According to the results of the monitoring, it is possible to interpret that the DDoS attack detection and mitigation mechanism implemented in the SDN controller is effective for TCP flood packet types, UDP flood, and ICMP flood are that detection is independent of the type of attack packet.

When an analysis of the associated approach to its counterparts is considered and knowing that OpenFlow entries are used to mitigate the attack. When the experimental results are compared to the results from the previous experiment, it is clear that the attack traffic with the preventive approach applied in this research can achieve a greater entropy decrease rate and has the function of quick detection. Table 4.2 lists the comparison between the proposed association method and its equivalent entropy method.

The test results of Figure 4.23 and 4.24 above demonstrate that the association entropy has a decent attack detection capability and can successfully capitalize the interconnection of information entropy and record energy entropy. It has a faster attack detection performance, although it has a high entropy packet loss rate, which is much better than other approaches, indicating that the methodology can identify DDoS attacks in simulated network circumstances.

Table 4.2: Comparative analysis of methods.

	Entropy Method		Association Method	
Attack traffic To Normal Traffic Ratio	Total Packets	Detection and Mitigation Time(s)	Total Packets	Detection and Mitigation Time(s)
25%	602	4	36	2
50%	548	6	77	2
75%	615	8	70	6
100%	750	4	122	2

Figure 4.23: Packets received and the ratio of attack traffic.

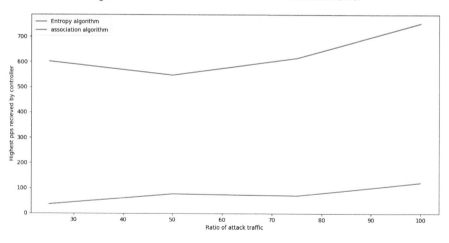

72

Figure 4.24: Time comparison to detect and mitigate the attack.

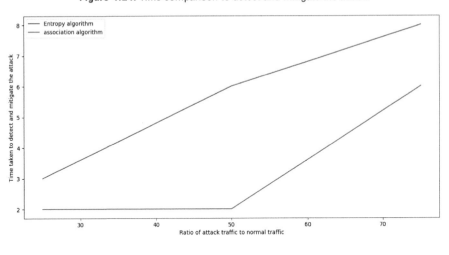

The generalized entropy-based approach with a dynamic threshold to detect DDoS attacks against a software-defined networking controller (GEADDDC) has been proposed in by Aladaileh (2021) to address the need. The experiment results prove that the GEADDDC effectively detects low-rate and high-rate DDoS attacks against the SDN controller that targets single or multiple victims. GEADDDC achieved it by generalizing the Rényi joint entropy to calculate incoming traffic's randomness using a statistic analyzer at the controller (Aladaileh, 2021). Meanwhile its failed to achieve some potential works includes exploring the feasibility of detecting additional types of DDoS attacks, such as TCP sync, ICMP, and HTTP flooding attacks; detecting DDoS attacks during flash crowd events; and integrating the proposed approach with other network security approaches. In Aladaileh (2021) the parameter UDP considered at large by providing multiple sources and multiple victims. For this work's comparison purpose single source and multiple victims can be taken. In this scenario Aladaileh (2021) achieves 1.39% false positive and 98.6% detection rate only for UDP and failed to answer how much time it takes. Meanwhile this work gains 4% and 96% for all flood attacks respectively and takes 2 s to be detected. This paper strongly suggests using destination IP address as a packet header in terms of reality because we do not get a clear information about the source, i.e., we do not know where it comes even the attacker can hide its IP address. The above experimental results show that the association entropy not only has a good attack detection performance but also can mitigate the attack and can effectively make use of the complementarity of information entropy. It not only has a fast attack detection speed, but also has a high entropy decline rate, which is significantly improved compared with other methods, which indicates the method can well detect DDoS attacks in simulated network scenarios.

The association entropy has the advantages of rapid detection and obvious changes in entropy value, which can be used in attacks. The attack is detected in the fastest time. At the same time, the entropy value when the attack comes is about 96% lower than the entropy value in the normal scenario, which can effectively detect the attack. Compared with other attack detection methods, it has great advantages in protecting SDN controller from DDoS attack. The implemented method is effective for TCP, UDP and ICMP flood DDoS attacks and meets the stated objectives.

The implemented security solution has been validated in this research by simulating Mininet and generating different packet flood attacks, which has contributed to a high level of effectiveness by selecting the appropriate entropy threshold to detect a DDoS attack. After applying this security solution in the simulation scenario, it coincides with the results of previous research allowing early detection for DDoS attacks and is effective with any type of packet (TCP, UDP, and ICMP).

Here controlled attacks were carried out for the monitoring process, because it is a simulated environment and it is not possible to have real attacks. The application of this process in a real-world environment does not require the generation of attacks by the organization, but rather the monitoring of its performance in the face of common events that occur in the network during a time period specified in the planning. This would provide in more accurate results for the solution's performance reporting.

The implemented system manages to achieve the stated objectives; however, it makes it difficult for the network administrator to represent the point at which the attack occurred and was mitigated, because this alert is lost in the controller terminal due to an excessive number of messages, indicating the network's current entropy. This also prevents further incidences in the controller from being discovered, making it impossible to monitor such devices and, as a result, the network. The solution was successful for the scenario proposed with the POX controller; however, there was little information found for other controllers.

The SDN design decouples the control plane from the data plane, making network reconfiguration and centralized management easier. However, due to the centralized nature of the SDN, the controller becomes a single point of failure that may be targeted by DDoS attacks, exposing the entire network. A conceptual methodology for safeguarding SDN networks, as well as a new technique for detecting and mitigating DDoS attacks, are discussed in this research. The execution of a DDoS attack directed at the SDN controller is rather simple and clear in that no unique packet type is required for the attack, since any of the UDP, TCP, or ICMP protocols may be used to flood the controller and analyze its resources. The suggested technique computes the number of DST_IPs associated with a single SRC_IP as well as the number of SRC_IPs associated with a single MAC_ADDR. Then it compares the computed values to the threshold values and adds the necessary flow entries.

The successful application of each fabric of the methodology resulted in the implementation of a solution based on network entropy calculation, capable of detecting UDP flood, TCP flood, and ICMP flood attacks early on and mitigating them by blocking the switch port from which the malicious traffic originates. Implementing the controller module solution saves money since the organization does not need to purchase additional software or hardware because the solution is based on open source. The implementation of the selected method is not necessarily complex, and making more advanced adjustments requires knowledge of the Python programming language even if you have basic understanding of how to use the POX controller. Network entropy is a value that may be used to detect anomalies in network traffic, in this example recognizing that a host is receiving an unusually large number of packets in comparison to the other hosts on the network. The solution achieves the objective of detecting and mitigating DDoS attacks on the network; however, the action of blocking the switch port connected to the host that performs the attack has the disadvantage that does not allow such a host to send or receive legitimate traffic.

As an improvement for this problem, Machine learning techniques could be implemented to filter the packets, so that the host is not blocked in its entirely, only the malicious traffic it generates. The simulation results showed that the proposed approach is successful for detecting the attack in a shorter period of time and with a low number of packets. Using flow entries, the attack is successfully mitigated after discovery. Using the POX controller has the benefit of previously having been thoroughly evaluated due to its open distribution, therefore there is a source of knowledge available on the solutions that can be developed with it, as opposed to other controllers whose information is rare.

It's advisable to make no configurations on the POX controller module l3 learning because if it has an error the client will not start; instead, make a duplicate of the file and build the configurations on this and choose a method with extensive theoretical and, more importantly, practical documentation to ensure that all necessary information is available at the time of deployment. It is recommended that a reasonable time be set aside to complete each subprocess, based on the availability of professionals and the resources needed to carry out the optimization method.

The work discussed is confined to the network layer, that is, it only evaluates the IP as a parameter for attack detection. In the future, this study might be expanded to include features from other layers, such as MAC addresses in the data link layer.

In addition, a load balancing module may also be built on a pool of controllers to further redistribute risk and efficiently manage traffic to the controller. It is also recommended to implement the GNS3 tool. Complex network topologies may be built with this tool. The simulation of multiple platforms is simple. The virtual network can be linked to the actual world.

References

[1]   Aladaileh, M., Anbar, M., Hasbullah, I. H., Sanjalawe, Y. K., & Chong, Y.-W. (2021). Entropy-based approach to detect DDoS attacks on software defined networking controller. CMC-COMPUTERS MATERIALS & CONTINUA, 69(1), 373-391.

5

Future Directions

The dynamic nature of software-defined networking (SDN) demands a forward-thinking approach to security. This chapter takes you beyond the present, exploring the frontiers of security solutions designed to anticipate and counter emerging threats in the ever-evolving cybersecurity landscape. This chapter also delves into the art of predicting future threats, analyzing trends, and understanding the evolving methodologies of attackers. By equipping you with the ability to anticipate the next wave of security challenges, you gain a strategic advantage in proactively strengthening your defenses. Next, we shift focus to the crucial concept of adaptive security measures. As threats evolve, static security solutions become obsolete. This chapter emphasizes the need for dynamic security mechanisms that can adjust and respond in real-time to new attack vectors and vulnerabilities. Understanding and implementing these adaptive solutions empowers you to maintain a resilient security posture in the face of continuous change. Finally, we unveil the transformative potential of artificial intelligence (AI) and machine learning (ML) in shaping the future of SDN security. Witness how these advanced technologies are revolutionizing defense mechanisms, enabling real-time threat detection, automated incident response, and continuous adaptation to the ever-shifting threat landscape. By exploring the integration of AI and ML, you gain valuable insights into the future of SDN security and its potential to safeguard your network infrastructure against even the most sophisticated attacks. This chapter serves as a beacon, guiding security professionals, network architects, and researchers towards a future-proof approach to SDN security.

5.1 Anticipating Emerging Threats

In the ever-evolving landscape of cybersecurity, anticipating emerging threats is paramount to staying ahead of cyber adversaries. As technology continues to advance at a rapid pace, new attack vectors and vulnerabilities inevitably emerge, presenting novel challenges for organizations worldwide. One area of concern lies in the proliferation of emerging technologies, such as the Internet of Things (IoT), 5G networks, and quantum computing, which bring unparalleled connectivity and capabilities but also introduce new avenues for exploitation. Additionally, the rise of nation-state threat actors leveraging cyberspace for espionage, sabotage, and geopolitical influence poses a significant risk to both public and private sector entities. With geopolitical tensions on the rise, the sophistication and frequency of nation-state-sponsored cyberattacks are expected to increase, underscoring the need for robust defense strategies. Furthermore, supply chain risks have become increasingly prominent, with cybercriminals targeting third-party vendors and service providers to gain access to sensitive data and systems. As evidenced by recent high-profile incidents, such as the SolarWinds supply chain attack, supply chain compromises can have far-reaching consequences, highlighting the importance of supply chain risk management and resilience. Moreover, the pervasive threat of ransomware continues to loom large, with cybercriminals employing increasingly sophisticated tactics, such as double extortion and ransomware-as-a-service (RaaS), to extort organizations for financial gain. As AI and machine learning technologies become more prevalent in cybersecurity defenses, they also introduce new risks, such as adversarial machine learning and AI-driven social engineering attacks. Thus, organizations must remain vigilant and proactive in their approach to cybersecurity, leveraging threat intelligence, adopting a defense-in-depth strategy, and investing in emerging technologies to stay one step ahead of cyber threats.

In addition to the aforementioned emerging threats, organizations must also contend with the evolving landscape of cybercrime, where cybercriminals continuously innovate and adapt their tactics to bypass traditional security measures. One such area of concern is the rise of sophisticated social engineering attacks, where cybercriminals exploit human psychology and behavioral patterns to manipulate individuals into divulging sensitive information or performing actions that compromise security. These attacks often leverage psychological triggers, such as fear, urgency, or curiosity, to deceive unsuspecting users and gain unauthorized access to systems or data. Moreover, as organizations increasingly rely on cloud services and digital transformation initiatives, they face new challenges related to cloud security and data privacy. Cloud-based threats, such as misconfigured cloud storage, insecure APIs, and unauthorized access to cloud resources, pose significant risks to organizations' data integrity and confidentiality. Additionally, the proliferation of interconnected devices in the Internet of Things (IoT) ecosystem introduces new attack surfaces and vulnerabilities, creating opportunities for cybercriminals to launch large-scale botnet attacks, data breaches, and distributed denial of service (DDoS) attacks. Furthermore, the growing complexity of IT environments, characterized by hybrid and multi-cloud architectures, containerized applications, and decentralized networks, presents challenges in managing security policies and enforcing consistent security controls across disparate environments. As organizations navigate these emerging threats and complexities, it is imperative to adopt a proactive and adaptive approach to cybersecurity, encompassing threat intelligence, security awareness training, robust access controls, and continuous monitoring and response capabilities. By staying informed about emerging threats, investing in cybersecurity best practices, and fostering a culture of security awareness, organizations can better safeguard their digital assets and mitigate the risks posed by evolving cyber threats.

Furthermore, the rapid pace of technological innovation, coupled with the increasing interconnectedness of digital ecosystems, has fueled the proliferation of cyber threats that transcend traditional boundaries. Advanced persistent threats (APTs), for instance, represent a persistent and stealthy form of cyberattack orchestrated by highly sophisticated threat actors, often with nation-state backing or criminal intent. These adversaries employ a range of tactics, techniques, and procedures (TTPs) to infiltrate target networks, evade detection, and exfiltrate sensitive information over extended periods. Moreover, as organizations embrace digital transformation initiatives and adopt emerging technologies such as artificial intelligence (AI), Internet of Things (IoT), and edge computing, they inadvertently expand their attack surface and introduce new vectors for exploitation. For example, AI-driven attacks, such as AI-generated deepfakes and AI-powered malware, pose unique challenges to traditional security defenses by leveraging machine learning algorithms to automate and enhance the effectiveness of cyberattacks. Similarly, the proliferation of IoT devices, characterized by diverse hardware, firmware, and communication protocols, introduces complexities in managing security vulnerabilities and ensuring device integrity across heterogeneous environments. Additionally, the rapid adoption of remote work and virtual collaboration tools in response to the COVID-19 pandemic has further amplified cybersecurity risks, as threat actors exploit vulnerabilities in remote access technologies, phishing emails, and insecure home networks to compromise corporate systems and steal sensitive data. In light of these emerging threats and challenges, organizations must adopt a holistic approach to cybersecurity that encompasses threat intelligence, risk management, proactive defense strategies, and collaborative partnerships with industry peers and cybersecurity experts. By fostering a culture of cybersecurity resilience and innovation, organizations can adapt to the evolving threat landscape and effectively mitigate the risks posed by emerging cyber threats.

Additionally, the convergence of physical and digital environments, often referred to as the Internet of Everything (IoE), introduces new complexities in securing critical infrastructure, smart cities, and interconnected supply chains. Threats to critical infrastructure, such as energy grids, transportation systems, and healthcare facilities, pose significant risks to public safety, economic stability, and national security. Similarly, the digitization of supply chains, characterized by globalized sourcing, real-time tracking, and interconnected logistics networks, presents opportunities for cyber adversaries to disrupt operations, steal intellectual property, and undermine trust in global commerce. Moreover, the proliferation of cyber warfare tactics, including offensive cyber operations, information warfare, and state-sponsored cyberattacks, underscores the need for international collaboration, diplomacy, and collective defense measures to deter malicious actors and safeguard the integrity of cyberspace. In conclusion, as organizations navigate the complex and dynamic landscape of emerging cyber threats, it is essential to prioritize resilience, agility, and collaboration in their cybersecurity strategies. By embracing a proactive and adaptive approach to cybersecurity, leveraging emerging technologies, and fostering a culture of cybersecurity awareness and innovation, organizations can effectively mitigate the risks posed by emerging cyber threats and safeguard their digital assets, critical infrastructure, and strategic interests in an increasingly interconnected world.

5.2 Adaptive Security Measures

Adaptive security measures represent a proactive and dynamic approach to cybersecurity, designed to anticipate, detect, and respond to evolving threats in real-time. Unlike traditional security approaches that rely on static defenses and predefined rulesets, adaptive security measures leverage advanced technologies such as artificial intelligence (AI), machine learning (ML), and behavioral analytics to continuously assess risks, adapt security controls, and mitigate emerging threats. By analyzing vast amounts of data, including network traffic patterns, user behavior, and threat intelligence feeds, adaptive security solutions can identify anomalies, suspicious activities, and potential security breaches with greater accuracy and speed than traditional methods.

Moreover, adaptive security measures enable organizations to automate incident response processes, orchestrate security workflows, and prioritize remediation efforts based on the severity and impact of detected threats. This proactive and agile approach to cybersecurity not only strengthens defenses against known threats but also enhances resilience against unknown and zero-day attacks, which may exploit previously unidentified vulnerabilities or bypass traditional security controls. Furthermore, adaptive security measures enable organizations to adapt their security posture in real-time based on changing business requirements, regulatory compliance mandates, and emerging cyber threats, ensuring a holistic and adaptive approach to cybersecurity risk management.

By embracing adaptive security measures, organizations can stay ahead of cyber adversaries, minimize the impact of security incidents, and maintain the integrity, confidentiality, and availability of their digital assets in an increasingly dynamic and complex threat landscape. In addition to their proactive and dynamic nature, adaptive security measures also promote a shift from a perimeter-based security paradigm to a more holistic and risk-based approach. Rather than relying solely on traditional perimeter defenses to protect against external threats, adaptive security measures recognize that the threat landscape extends beyond the network perimeter and encompasses a diverse range of attack vectors, including insider threats, supply chain risks, and third-party vulnerabilities. As a result, adaptive security solutions prioritize continuous monitoring, visibility, and threat intelligence across the entire digital ecosystem, including cloud environments, endpoints, applications, and IoT devices. By adopting a risk-based approach to cybersecurity, organizations can allocate resources more effectively, focus on mitigating the most critical threats, and align security investments with business objectives and regulatory requirements. Furthermore, adaptive security measures enable organizations to adapt their security controls and policies dynamically in response to changing threat landscapes, compliance mandates, and operational requirements. This flexibility and agility empower organizations to strike a balance between security and usability, allowing them to innovate and grow without compromising on cybersecurity resilience. Ultimately, by embracing adaptive security measures as a core tenet of their cybersecurity strategy, organizations can build a robust defense posture that evolves in lockstep with the ever-changing cyber threat landscape, ensuring long-term resilience and protection against emerging threats.

Adaptive security measures encompass a range of techniques and technologies aimed at enhancing an organization's ability to detect, respond to, and recover from cybersecurity threats in real-time. One key aspect of adaptive security is its reliance on advanced analytics and machine learning algorithms to analyze vast amounts of data and identify patterns indicative of potential security incidents or anomalies. By leveraging these capabilities, organizations can detect threats more quickly and accurately than traditional signature-based approaches, which rely on predefined patterns of known threats. Additionally, adaptive security measures often incorporate behavior-based anomaly detection, which involves establishing a baseline of normal behavior for users, devices, and applications, and flagging deviations from this baseline as potential security risks. This approach allows organizations to detect insider threats, compromised accounts, and other malicious activities that may evade traditional security controls.

Moreover, adaptive security measures prioritize continuous monitoring and visibility across the entire digital infrastructure, including cloud environments, endpoints, networks, and IoT devices. This comprehensive approach enables organizations to gain a holistic view of their security posture and identify vulnerabilities or misconfigurations that could be exploited by cyber adversaries. Additionally, adaptive security solutions often integrate threat intelligence feeds from multiple sources, including industry consortiums, government agencies, and commercial vendors, to stay abreast of the latest threats and attack techniques.

Another key aspect of adaptive security is its emphasis on automation and orchestration of security processes. By automating routine tasks such as threat detection, incident response, and remediation, organizations can reduce response times, minimize human error, and improve overall operational efficiency. Furthermore, adaptive security solutions often employ dynamic policy enforcement mechanisms that adjust security controls in real-time based on changing risk factors, such as user behavior, network conditions, and threat intelligence feeds. This adaptability allows organizations to tailor their security posture to specific threats and vulnerabilities, ensuring a more effective defense against emerging cyber threats. adaptive security measures represent a proactive, holistic, and dynamic approach to cybersecurity that leverages advanced analytics, continuous monitoring, threat intelligence, and automation to detect, respond to, and mitigate cybersecurity threats in real-time. By embracing adaptive security principles, organizations can enhance their resilience to cyber-attacks, minimize the impact of security incidents, and maintain the integrity, confidentiality, and availability of their digital assets in an increasingly complex and evolving threat landscape.

Adaptive security solutions often integrate with other security tools and platforms to provide a holistic and coordinated approach to cybersecurity. Collaboration with industry peers, government agencies, and cybersecurity experts is also crucial for sharing threat intelligence, best practices, and lessons learned, thereby enhancing collective defense against cyber threats.

By implementing adaptive security measures, organizations can enhance their resilience to cyber-attacks, minimize the impact of security incidents, and maintain the integrity, confidentiality, and availability of their digital assets in an increasingly complex and evolving threat landscape.

In conclusion, the adoption of adaptive security measures is essential for organizations seeking to effectively mitigate the risks posed by the rapidly evolving cyber threat landscape. By embracing advanced analytics, continuous monitoring, and automation, organizations can enhance their ability to detect, respond to, and recover from cybersecurity threats in real-time. Moreover, adaptive security solutions enable organizations to prioritize resources, focus on mitigating the most critical threats, and align security investments with business objectives and regulatory requirements. Furthermore, the shift towards a risk-based approach to cybersecurity allows organizations to strike a balance between security and usability, fostering innovation and growth without compromising on cybersecurity resilience. Ultimately, by embracing adaptive security measures as a core tenet of their cybersecurity strategy, organizations can build a robust defense posture that evolves in tandem with the ever-changing threat landscape, ensuring long-term resilience and protection against emerging cyber threats.

5.3 The Role of AI and Machine Learning

The role of artificial intelligence (AI) and machine learning (ML) in cybersecurity is becoming increasingly significant as organizations seek more proactive and adaptive approaches to defending against cyber threats. AI and ML technologies enable cybersecurity systems to analyze vast amounts of data, identify patterns, and detect anomalies indicative of potential security incidents or malicious activities in real-time. By leveraging these capabilities, organizations can enhance their ability to detect and respond to cyber threats more effectively, often detecting threats that may have gone unnoticed by traditional security measures. Furthermore, AI and ML algorithms can continuously learn and evolve based on new data and emerging threats, improving the accuracy and efficiency of cybersecurity defenses over time. Additionally, AI-powered tools can automate routine security tasks, such as threat detection, incident response, and vulnerability management, allowing cybersecurity teams to focus on more strategic initiatives and higher-level decision-making. Moreover, AI-driven security solutions can help organizations adapt to the rapidly changing threat landscape by providing timely threat intelligence, predictive analytics, and proactive risk management capabilities. Overall, the integration of AI and ML technologies into cybersecurity operations is essential for organizations looking to stay ahead of cyber adversaries, minimize the impact of security incidents, and maintain the integrity and confidentiality of their digital assets in an increasingly complex and dynamic threat environment.

In addition to their role in threat detection and response, AI and machine learning technologies are also revolutionizing other areas of cybersecurity. One significant area is in predictive analytics, where AI algorithms analyze historical data to forecast future cyber threats and trends. By identifying patterns and correlations in past security incidents, organizations can anticipate potential attack vectors, vulnerabilities, and tactics used by cyber adversaries, enabling them to proactively implement preventive measures and strengthen their defenses. Moreover, AI-driven risk assessment tools can help organizations prioritize security investments and allocate resources more effectively by quantifying the likelihood and potential impact of various cyber threats. Furthermore, AI and ML techniques are increasingly being applied to enhance user authentication and access control mechanisms. Behavioral biometrics, for example, analyze user behavior patterns to verify identity and detect anomalies that may indicate unauthorized access or account compromise. Similarly, AI-powered identity and access management (IAM) systems can dynamically adjust user privileges and permissions based on risk factors and contextual information, reducing the likelihood of insider threats and credential-based attacks. Overall, the role of AI and machine learning in cybersecurity is multifaceted, encompassing threat detection, predictive analytics, risk assessment, and access control, among other areas. As organizations continue to embrace digital transformation and face increasingly sophisticated cyber threats, AI and ML technologies will play a crucial role in enabling proactive and adaptive cybersecurity defenses that can keep pace with the evolving threat landscape.

Threat detection and response: AI and machine learning algorithms play a pivotal role in detecting and responding to cyber threats in real-time. These technologies can analyze vast amounts of data from various sources, including network traffic, system logs, and user behavior, to identify patterns and anomalies indicative of potential security incidents. By leveraging advanced analytics and anomaly detection techniques, AI-powered security systems can differentiate between normal and suspicious activities, enabling organizations to respond promptly to emerging threats.

Predictive analytics and threat intelligence: AI-driven predictive analytics leverage historical data and machine learning algorithms to forecast future cyber threats and trends. By analyzing patterns and correlations in past security incidents, organizations can anticipate potential attack vectors, vulnerabilities, and tactics used by cyber adversaries, enabling them to proactively implement preventive measures and strengthen their defenses. Moreover, AI-powered threat intelligence platforms aggregate and analyze data from multiple sources, including open-source intelligence (OSINT), dark web forums, and security research reports, to provide organizations with timely and actionable insights into emerging cyber threats.

Risk assessment and prioritization: AI and machine learning techniques are also employed in risk assessment and prioritization, helping organizations quantify the likelihood and potential impact of various cyber threats. AI-driven risk assessment tools analyze data from multiple sources, including vulnerability scans, security logs, and threat intelligence feeds, to identify and prioritize security risks based on their severity, likelihood, and potential impact on business operations. By prioritizing security investments and allocating resources more effectively, organizations can mitigate the most critical threats and vulnerabilities first, reducing their overall cyber risk exposure.

User authentication and access control: AI and machine learning technologies are increasingly being applied to enhance user authentication and access control mechanisms. Behavioral biometrics, for example, analyze user behavior patterns, such as typing speed, mouse movements, and navigation patterns, to verify identity and detect anomalies that may indicate unauthorized access or account compromise. Similarly, AI-powered identity and access management (IAM) systems can dynamically adjust user privileges and permissions based on risk factors and contextual information, reducing the likelihood of insider threats and credential-based attacks.

Automation and orchestration: AI-driven automation and orchestration capabilities streamline security operations by automating routine tasks, such as threat detection, incident response, and vulnerability management. By leveraging AI-powered security orchestration, automation, and response (SOAR) platforms, organizations can accelerate incident detection and response times, minimize human error, and improve overall operational efficiency. Moreover, AI-driven security automation enables organizations to scale their security operations effectively, even in the face of limited resources and increasing workloads.

Adaptive and context-aware defenses: AI and machine learning technologies enable organizations to develop adaptive and context-aware cybersecurity defenses that can dynamically adjust security controls and policies based on changing threat landscapes, compliance mandates, and operational requirements. By analyzing contextual information, such as user behavior, network conditions, and threat intelligence feeds, AI-powered security systems can tailor their responses to specific threats and vulnerabilities, ensuring a more effective defense against emerging cyber threats.

Overall, the role of AI and machine learning in cybersecurity is multifaceted, encompassing threat detection, predictive analytics, risk assessment, access control, automation, and adaptive defenses. As organizations continue to face increasingly sophisticated cyber threats and embrace digital transformation initiatives, AI and ML technologies will play an increasingly crucial role in enabling proactive and adaptive cybersecurity defenses that can keep pace with the evolving threat landscape.

References

[1]   Aladaileh, M., Anbar, M., Hasbullah, I. H., Sanjalawe, Y. K., & Chong, Y.-W. (2021). Entropy-based approach to detect DDoS attacks on software defined networking controller. CMC-COMPUTERS MATERIALS & CONTINUA, 69(1), 373-391.

[2]   AbdelAzim, N. M., Fahmy, S. F., Sobh, M. A., & Eldin, A. M. B. (2021). A hybrid entropy-based DoS attacks detection system for software defined networks (SDN): A proposed trust mechanism. Egyptian Informatics Journal, 22(1), 85-90.

[3]   Abdullah, M. Z., Al-awad, N. A., & Hussein, F. W. (2019). Evaluating and Comparing the Performance of Using Multiple Controllers in Software Defined Networks. International Journal of Modern Education & Computer Science, 11(8).

[4]   AL-Musawi, B. Q. M. (2012). Mitigating DoS/DDoS attacks using iptables. International Journal of Engineering & Technology, 12(3), 101-111.

[5]   Aladaileh, M., Anbar, M., Hasbullah, I. H., Sanjalawe, Y. K., & Chong, Y.-W. (2021). Entropy-based approach to detect DDoS attacks on software defined networking controller. CMC-COMPUTERS MATERIALS & CONTINUA, 69(1), 373-391.

[6]   Anthony, L. (2015). Security Risks in SDN and Other New Software Issues. RSA Conference. Frost and Sullivan,

[7]   Bannour, F., Souihi, S., & Mellouk, A. (2017). Distributed SDN control: Survey, taxonomy, and challenges. IEEE Communications Surveys & Tutorials, 20(1), 333-354.

[8]   Bouras, C., Kollia, A., & Papazois, A. (2017). Teaching network security in mobile 5G using ONOS SDN controller. 2017 Ninth International Conference on Ubiquitous and Future Networks (ICUFN),

[9]   Cui, Y., Qian, Q., Guo, C., Shen, G., Tian, Y., Xing, H., & Yan, L. (2021). Towards DDoS detection mechanisms in software-defined networking. Journal of Network and computer Applications, 103156.

[10] Dao, N.-N., Kim, J., Park, M., & Cho, S. (2016). Adaptive suspicious prevention for defending DoS attacks in SDN-based convergent networks. PloS one, 11(8), e0160375.

[11] DeCusatis, C., Carranza, A., & Delgado-Caceres, J. (2016). Modeling Software Defined Networks using Mininet. Proc. 2nd Int. Conf. Comput. Inf. Sci. Technol. Ottawa, Canada,

[12] Deepa, V., Sudar, K. M., & Deepalakshmi, P. (2019). Design of ensemble learning methods for DDoS detection in SDN environment. 2019 International Conference on Vision Towards Emerging Trends in Communication and Networking (ViTECoN),

[13] Dharma, N. G., Muthohar, M. F., Prayuda, J. A., Priagung, K., & Choi, D. (2015). Time-based DDoS detection and mitigation for SDN controller. 2015 17th Asia-Pacific Network Operations and Management Symposium (APNOMS),

[14] Dong, S., Abbas, K., & Jain, R. (2019). A survey on distributed denial of service (DDoS) attacks in SDN and cloud computing environments. IEEE Access, 7, 80813-80828.

[15] Emmons, m. a. (2021). ScapyPacket Manipulation in Kali Linux. geeksforgeeks.org. Retrieved 15 Apr, 2022 from https://www.geeksforgeeks.org/scapy-packet-manipulation-in-kali-linux/

[16] Glvan, D., Rcuciu, C., Moinescu, R., & Antonie, N.-F. (2019). Detecting the DDoS attack for SDN Controller. Scientific Bulletin" Mircea cel Batran" Naval Academy, 22(1), 1-8.

[17] Hadi, F., Imran, M., Durad, M. H., & Waris, M. (2018). A simple security policy enforcement system for an institution using SDN controller. 2018 15th International Bhurban Conference on Applied Sciences and Technology (IBCAST),

[18] Hameed, S., & Ahmed Khan, H. (2018). SDN based collaborative scheme for mitigation of DDoS attacks. Future Internet, 10(3), 23.

[19] Haque, M. R., Tan, S. C., Lee, C. K., Yusoff, Z., Ali, S., Kaspin, I., & Ziri, S. R. (2018). Analysis of DDoS attack-aware software-defined networking controller placement in Malaysia. In Recent Trends in Computer Applications (pp. 175-188). Springer.

[20] Haque, M. R., Tan, S. C., Yusoff, Z., Nisar, K., Lee, C. K., Kaspin, R., Chowdhry, B. S., Ali, S., & Memon, S. (2020). A Novel DDoS Attack-aware Smart Backup Controller Placement in SDN Design.

Annals of Emerging Technologies in Computing (AETiC), Print ISSN, 2516-0281.

[21] Jose, A. S., Nair, L. R., & Paul, V. (2021). Towards Detecting Flooding DDOS Attacks Over Software Defined Networks Using Machine Learning Techniques.REVISTAGEINTEC-GESTAOINOVETECNOLOGIAS, 11(4), 3837-3865.

[22] Kalkan, K., & Zeadally, S. (2017). Securing internet of things with software defined networking. IEEE Communications Magazine, 56(9), 186-192.

[23] Kandoi, R., & Antikainen, M. (2015). Denial-of-service attacks in OpenFlow SDN networks. 2015 IFIP/IEEE International Symposium on Integrated Network Management (IM),

[24] Kodzai, C. (2020). Impact of network security on SDN controller performance University of Cape Town.

[25] Kreutz, D., Ramos, F. M., & Verissimo, P. (2013). Towards secure and dependable software-defined networks. Proceedings of the second ACM SIGCOMM workshop on Hot topics in software defined networking,

[26] Kreutz, D., Ramos, F. M., Verissimo, P. E., Rothenberg, C. E., Azodolmolky, S., & Uhlig, S. (2014). Software-defined networking: A comprehensive survey. Proceedings of the IEEE, 103(1), 14-76.

[27] Lawal, B. H., & Nuray, A. (2018). Real-time detection and mitigation of distributed denial of service (DDoS) attacks in software defined networking (SDN). 2018 26th Signal Processing and Communications Applications Conference (SIU),

[28] Masoudi, R., & Ghaffari, A. (2016). Software defined networks: A survey. Journal of Network and computer Applications, 67, 1-25.

[29] Mishra, A., Gupta, N., & Gupta, B. (2021). Defense mechanisms against DDoS attack based on entropy in SDN-cloud using POX controller. Telecommunication systems, 77(1), 47-62.

[30] Mladenov, B. (2019). Studying the DDoS attack effect over SDN controller southbound channel. 2019 X National Conference with International Participation (ELECTRONICA),

[31] Mousavi, S. M., & St-Hilaire, M. (2018). Early detection of DDoS attacks against software defined network controllers. Journal of Network and Systems Management, 26(3), 573-591.

[32] Patel, P. (July 5, 2016). Implementing software defined network (SDN) based firewall. Nirma University. Retrieved April 19, 2022, https://www.opensourceforu.com/2016/07/implementing-a-software-defined-network-sdn-based-firewall/

[33] Sahoo, K. S., Sarkar, A., Mishra, S. K., Sahoo, B., Puthal, D., Obaidat, M. S., & Sadun, B. (2017). Metaheuristic solutions for solving controller

placement problem in SDN-based WAN architecture. ICETE 2017-Proceedings of the 14th International Joint Conference on e-Business and Telecommunications,

[34]   Sakellaropoulou, D. (2017). A qualitative study of sdn controllers. Athens University of Economics and Business.

[35]   Salman, O., Elhajj, I. H., Kayssi, A., & Chehab, A. (2016). SDN controllers: A comparative study. 2016 18th mediterranean electrotechnical conference (MELECON),

[36]   Shohani, R. B., Mostafavi, S., & Hakami, V. (2021). A statistical model for early detection of DDoS attacks on random targets in SDN. Wireless Personal Communications, 120(1), 379-400.

[37]   Stallings, W. (2015). Foundations of modern networking: SDN, NFV, QoE, IoT, and Cloud. Addison-Wesley Professional.

[38]   Thomas, R. M., & James, D. (2017). DDOS detection and denial using third party application in SDN. 2017 International Conference on Energy, Communication, Data Analytics and Soft Computing (ICECDS),

[39]   Wang, R., Jia, Z., & Ju, L. (2015). An entropy-based distributed DDoS detection mechanism in software-defined networking. 2015 IEEE Trustcom/BigDataSE/ISPA,

[40]   Yu, S., Zhang, J., Liu, J., Zhang, X., Li, Y., & Xu, T. (2021). A cooperative DDoS attack detection scheme based on entropy and ensemble learning in SDN. EURASIP Journal on Wireless Communications and Networking, 2021(1), 1-21.

APPENDICES

A1. Set up and Configuration

This section includes and provides further information on the specifications and customization settings of the tools used in the book's experiments. The specific details will give the reader with the installation processes, setup technique, and configurations that were used to deliver the proposed solution.

A2. Prerequisites for Setting up an Environment

Virtual Box: Simply download the most recent version of Virtual Box for your operating system from the link: https://www.virtualbox.org/wiki/Downloads

Mininet: Mininet the packet forwarder emulation software is installed on Ubuntu server. The installation steps for the software are as shown below from Mininet website. Source of the packages is extracted from http://mininet.org/download/. The installation option that was used is the native installation from source option.

Scapy on Mininet: To install scapy manually type in the following command: $ sudo apt-get install python-scapy

Python on Mininet: If Python is not installed on Mininet, type in the following command to install it manually: $ sudo apt-get install python3

SDN Controller setup using POX: Move to the pox directory in the Virtual Box terminal running Mininet by entering the following command: $ cd pox

In the SSH window and terminal of Virtual Box enter the following command to run the pox controller: $ python3./pox.py forwarding. l3_editing

91

A3. Hardware Features Requirement

Table A3.1: Hardware features and roles.

Features	Detail
Processor	Intel®Core ™ i7-8565U CPU @ 1.80GHz 1.99GHz
RAM	12 GB
Hard disk	1.5 TB NV Me Solid State Drive (SSD)
Operating System	Windows®11 and Ubuntu 20.04 LTS
Wireless Network	Intel ®Dual Band Wireless-AC 8265

A4. Experimental Setup Server Features

Table A4.1: Virtual machine specifications and roles.

Specifications	Detail
Virtual Machine Name	Mininet + POX
Platform	Ubuntu
Version	Ubuntu (64-bit) 20.04 LTS
RAM	4096MB
Virtual Hard disk size	40 GB
Network Configuration	Bridged Adaptor
CPU	3 Cores

Index

Methodology to Improve Control Plane Security in SDN Environments

Wendwossen Desalegn | **Javed Shaikh** | **Bayisa Taye**

This book unveils a blueprint for safeguarding the very backbone of modern communication networks. It offers a roadmap towards fortifying SDN infrastructures against the relentless onslaught of cyber threats, ensuring resilience and reliability in an ever-evolving digital landscape.

This is an exhaustive study of crafting a robust security solution tailored for the SDN environment, specifically targeting the detection and mitigation of distributed denial of service (DDoS) attacks on the control plane. The methodology hinges on an early detection strategy, meticulously aligned with industry standards, serving as a beacon for professionals navigating the intricate realm of implementing security solutions. This reference elucidates an innovative approach devised to identify and mitigate the inherent risks associated with the OpenFlow protocol and its POX controller. Validated through rigorous simulations conducted within controlled environments utilizing the Mininet tool and SDN controller, the methodology unfolds, showcasing the intricate dance between theory and practice.

Through meticulous observation of detection algorithm results in simulated environments, followed by real-world implementation within network testbeds, the proposed solution emerges triumphant. Leveraging network entropy calculation, coupled with swift port blocking mechanisms, the methodology stands as a formidable barrier against a DDoS attack such as TCP, UDP, and ICMP floods.

Exclusively Distributed by

Routledge
Taylor & Francis Group
www.routledge.com

an **informa** business

River Publishers

978-87-7004-195-9

ONLINE LEARNING ANALYTICS

edited by
Jay Liebowitz

CRC Press
Taylor & Francis Group

AN AUERBACH BOOK